THE ART
OF FEAR-FREE LIVING

"Catrice M. Jackson does a wonderful job of encouraging her readers to claim their lives and step into their unique Genius. She blends powerful personal stories from her own and others' experience with specific questions and tools that will help people target the areas they need to address and move them toward a fear-free life. I love that she laid out the issue and then gave constructive ways for people to start to shift their thinking and take responsibility."

—Adee Swanson, MA
Certified Spirit Coach®
Illuminate the Genius Within

"Catrice M. Jackson excels at communicating the steps necessary to foster positive change in our lives. *The Art of Fear Free Living* approach addresses many of the blocks that allow fear to silence the voice of our soul. The altered dynamics of personal relationships is one factor that drives us to remain static and hinders the manifestation of our dreams. She clearly defines the process of increasing that circle of trusted friends that we all desire, while also making significant changes in our life path. Catrice addresses the necessity of letting go and the importance of living in the present. Her frank but eloquent prose offers practical contemplation and application. The fearless journey can be navigated and approaches like this are the key to guiding one another to a life of courage."

—Emily-Allison Tarapchak
Writer and Blogger, True for Now: 365 Days of Prose

"The chapter on prosperity hits to the core of the true definition of the word. Catrice has opened her own wound so that we, the reader, can become the students and learn from her "hard knocks" in life. Once we have gathered all the tools we need from observing and studying her lesson, she closes her wound and by the time we venture through Amethyst's story of finding her Divine Wealth, this wound has scarred but has not left any disfiguring results. It's just a mark big enough to remind her, and us, that "Your true prosperity lives in your soul.""

—Tamara Elizabeth
Master Motivator for Women in Transition
Certified Self-love Coach

"I didn't realize that I was letting my ego keep me small, often I think my ego is simply defined as me being too full of myself or giving too much advice and not using it myself, but after doing the exercises in this book I see the many facets of the ego and how incredibly sneaky the ego is. My ego tricks me into thinking its helping me, but in reality it is the sole reason for holding me back. Catrices' book, *The Art of Fear-Free Living*, really impacted my life. I've started relooking at my five year plan, and my goal is to make sure my ego has NO PART OF IT! I honestly believe that keeping my ego out of my five year plan will be my ticket to achieving all of it. Thanks to *The Art of Fear-Free Living*, I can silence my ShEgo and give power to my SHero!" Thank you Catrice. You are a good woman, making a difference in the lives of women, one heart at a time."

—*Andrea MacLeod*
Author of *Sister, We Need To Talk*
Founder of Womensville.com

"*The Art of Fear-Free Living* is a beautiful collection of stories by eleven very courageous women. This book gives you an intimate view of each woman's life and how they found the strength, power and faith to conquer the situations they found themselves in. It is filled with inspiration and practical tips on how to bust through your fears and start living your life on your terms."

—*Sherrie Koretke*
The Niche Clarity Coach

The Art of
Fear-Free Living

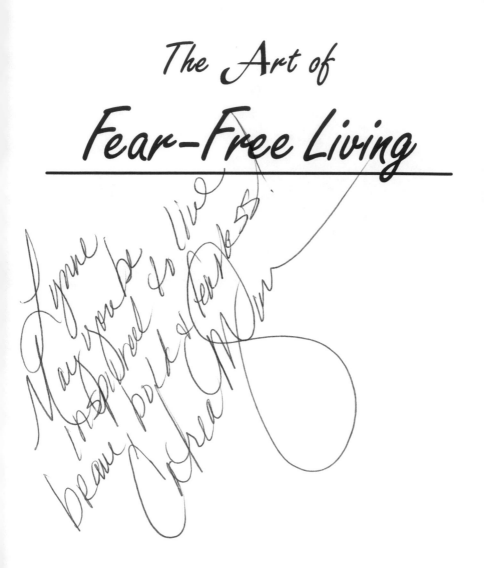

Lynne

May you be to live
inspired to live
brave, bold & fearless.

Andrea Aimi

OTHER FLAVORS
OF CATRICEOLOGY

Books

Delicious!
The Savvy Woman's Guide for Living a Sweet,
Sassy and Satisfied Life

Soul Eruption!
An Amazing Journey of Self Discovery

Life Empowerment Programs

The Art of Fear-Free Living
6-Week Audio/Video Telecourse

Courageous Conversations w/Catrice

The Fearlessly Delicious Life Radio Show

The Art of
Fear-Free Living

Awaken Your Geni(us)

CATRICE M. JACKSON

Emerge Consulting, LLC

Omaha, Nebraska

FOR INFORMATION CONTACT:
Catrice M. Jackson, M.S., LMHP, LPC
International Empowerment Speaker, Fear-Free Living Expert,
America's Delicious Life Designer and Author

Online ordering is available for all products.

Please visit our website at:
www.theartoffearfreeliving.com
www.catriceology.com

ISBN: 978-0-9838398-0-4
Library of Congress Control Number: 2011934536

Printed in the USA
10 9 8 7 6 5 4 3 2 1

CONTENTS

THE ART
OF FEAR-FREE LIVING

Awaken Your Geni(us)

—Catrice M. Jackson

Facing your fears is the doorway to freedom...
and courage is the key to unlocking your Genie

- Are you hiding behind masks and want to reveal the real you?
- Are your days filled with worry, doubt, emptiness, confusion and or fear?
- Do you have dreams but are afraid to take steps to make them a reality?
- Would you like leave your job and start a career that fulfills you?
- Are you afraid to let go of relationships that are toxic but really desire to?
- Would you like to be more brave, daring, confident and authentic in life?

If you answered yes to any of the above questions you have picked up the right book for the right moment... now.

It's time to awaken your Genius!

FEAR-FREE LIVING IS AN ART...

Living a courageous fear-free life is an art. It is an art because you are the co-creator of your life and the story you live comes to life by the power of your pen. Your pen (mind, spirit and actions) illustrate whether your life dances with colorful joy or is constricted with shades of black and white. It is an art because life is a blank canvas and you are the artist who with whatever tools you choose, you design it to portray what lies in your heart.

Living fear free is an art. It is an art because each person defines fear on their own terms and fear affects each of us differently. It is an art because fear and its manifestations in our life can often be abstract and only we know the true meaning behind the images on our canvas of life. The way we as individuals live our life is an art in itself and therefore living fear-free is an artistic representation of ourselves and how we choose to live. Prepare to embark upon a magical soul journey to discover, embrace, release, and celebrate the powerful brilliance of your inner Geni(us). Sprinkled with life empowerment tips, inspirational quotes and fearless living strategies, you'll be inspired to summon your inner Genie and courageously grant your every command and the desires of your heart. This is your gold-lantern moment to break free from the captivity of fear, re-create your life story and liberate your life and dreams. Hop on your magic carpet, take a deep breath, trust and believe in yourself and let the magical awakening begin.

Experience these magical moments...

- Discover how strong, brave and wise you are.
- Embrace the power of living in love instead of living in fear.
- Move from paralyzed to passionate, powerful and purposed.
- Receive the keys of clarity, confidence and courage to unlock your SHero.
- Diminish the power of fear and eliminate its grip on your life.
- Awaken the authentic, brilliant woman within and elevate to your highest self.

DEDICATION

This book is dedicated to the source of all my needs, wants and desires, the Almighty God. Nothing but the favor, mercy and grace of the Divine One kept me during this evolutionary moment of my life. When my days were dark he promised me sunshine. When my dreams were disappearing he promised me more than I could ever imagine. When I felt defeated and discouraged he promised me victory and joy. The God I serve does not make false promises and his mercy and grace endureth forever.

There were times when I cried alone in the dark, begging and pleading for deliverance from fear, doubt and worry. It was in those moments that I completely surrendered to God and his will and purpose for my life. There were moments when I didn't know how the bills were going to get paid and God always created a way out of no way by giving me what I needed when I needed it. There were moments when I wanted to give up, throw in the towel and walk away from my dreams and each time he whispered, "you of little faith, I will keep you and guide you but you must not give up." There were times when I felt like I was living a lie and questioned the purpose for my life.

In each of these often heart-breaking and humbling experiences I realized that I was being tested so that I could have a testimony. I realized that I was being humbled in my mess so it could be a message to inspire others wallowing in fear. There is absolutely no way I could have survived the valley moments without the grace of God, which I know for sure if I know nothing else. Through my pain I discovered real pleasure. Through my chaos I gained a deeper sense of clarity. Through my trials I know what it really feels like to be triumphant. Through it all I am wiser, stronger, more resilient and grateful to have been chosen to carry out a mission bigger than my wildest dreams. Today through deep gratitude, I rose from the ashes with wings spread wide and far committed to soaring fearlessly through my life, with no regret and inspiring others to do the same.

> *"I can do all things through Christ who strengthens me."*
>
> *Philippians 4:13*

I'd also like to dedicate this book to you and every woman in the world who has gone through the fire, is going through the fire or will go through the fire in life. This book is dedicated to every woman who thought she couldn't but she did, to every woman who didn't know how but found a way and to every woman who stood in the midst of fear and through faith and courage walked out fearless.

I am the woman I am today because of many factors, circumstances, events and experiences. I am the woman I am today because of the courageous decisions and actions of my mother, Robbie Jackson. Through her struggles and triumphs I learned that I too could be victorious in the midst of fear and strife. She never gave up, allowed me to be me and believed in me, my potential, and my gifts from the first day she laid eyes on me. She is my biggest fan! I love you mom and appreciate all the sacrifices you made for me.

One of the biggest fears I had in my life as a result of abandonment and not knowing who my real father is was having the ability to allow myself to love and be loved unconditionally. From my story you'll learn that men were not available, accountable, responsible, and/or present to the extent I believed they should be. I took a risk and allowed myself to be vulnerable to the deep experience of love. Love is not perfect and love can be a challenge yet when you allow yourself to freely experience, express and receive it is the most rewarding experience of a lifetime. Thank you Roy Jackson, my husband, for helping me face and conquer this fear, take the risk and know that I am worthy of love and all that it brings.

During my journey through fear there was always one bright light standing at the end of the tunnel, my son. I dedicate this book to you as you are a primary source of joy in my life. Although you are growing into a young man in my heart you will always be my little man. I thank you for choosing to come through me and choosing me as your mother. I never take for granted the privilege and honor to be your mother and know you are indeed a gift from God, one that I look forward to unwrapping time after time with the joyous anticipation of the first time. Thank you for blessing my life and allowing me to experience unconditional love in its purest form. You too are the wind beneath my wings. I love you more than words can express. No matter what valley you may find yourself in throughout your life know that your belief and faith in God will always be the compass to guide you back into the light. My hope for you is that you learn how to courageously face and conquer your fears and that you learn the lessons in the valley moments. God created you for a special mission and purpose in life and I pray that you allow his vision for your life to unfold before your eyes. When it is clearly revealed to you, rise up, take your place and courageously step into your divine greatness. Be brave, be fearless and faithfully fulfill God's destiny for your life.

I dedicate this book to every person who walked away, to every person who did not realize my value and to every person who was in my life for a reason or a season. Thank you for your lesson it allowed me to discover how wise, strong, resilient and brave I really am. This book is also dedicated to every person who believes in me, supports me and knows the value of who I am and the gifts I have to share with the world; for you will be with me for a life time and I am grateful for you. Thank you. I look forward our fearless journey together.

ACKNOWLEDGMENTS

Special thanks to eleven amazingly generous and fearless women who were brave enough to transparently share their stories in this book. Each of these brave women are living a courageous life because they've mastered *The Art of Fear-Free Living*. As heart-centered, conscious women and servants to the world they are dedicated to helping women in particular live fearless, satisfying, prosperous lives. I am deeply grateful and appreciate each of them for they are true champions for women and the wind beneath my wings.

Linda Joy
Aimee Yawnick
Lorna Blake
Amy Beth O'Brien
Angela Schaefers
Christina Morassi
Dr. Carla Goddard
Amethyst Wyldfyre
Christine Pembleton
Gayle Joplin Hall, PhD
Shann Vander Leek

Love, light and joy my fearless femmes!

FOREWORD

*"Each time we face our fear, we gain strength,
courage and confidence in the doing."*

—*Unknown*

As spiritual women living a human existence it's safe to say we've each experienced being pulled in opposite directions by two distinct and powerful forces within. At times these opposing forces can leave us feeling like an observer in our own life as each force struggles to be heard and expressed and the outcome of our lives are directed by which voice we listen to the most.

Catrice and her contributors come together to share one simple, yet powerful universal truth—the inner force (voice) that you choose to focus on has the power to either create or stifle the life of your dreams. Which voice do you feed?

Do you choose to honor the inner voice that uplifts, empowers and inspires you to create and live your unique purpose? A loving voice that supports and encourages you to connect with the Divine flow of life. A voice that guides you in bringing forth your unique vibrant essence. A voice that fills you with love, light and possibility.

Or do you find yourself choosing the insidious negative voice that fills you with self-doubt, fear, envy, indecision and procrastination thereby holding you back from living your dreams and fulfilling your soul's purpose? A voice that seems to feed off your most intimate feelings related to your self-worth and deservedness and thrives on keeping you from living our soul's purpose.

You hold the magic lamp to creating the life and inner tapestry of your dreams—it is the voice of love, the voice of your inner Geni(us) and its waiting for you to embrace its truth.

Like the inspiring women you will meet throughout the pages of this enlightening book I know only too well the paralyzing grip of fear as it held me captive in its embrace threatening to smother my dreams, my inner calling.

In my twenty year transformation from single, welfare mother to the leader in women's inspirational publishing I know first-hand the power of passion, courage, faith and perseverance in overcoming fearful thinking to achieve your dreams.

My greatest wish for each of you is that you embrace the truth of who you are and the unique gifts you bring to the world and allow your light to shine brightly. May the wisdom, insights and empowerment tools shared in *The Art of Fear-Free Living* provide you with the inspiration to break free from the captivity of fear and liberate your life and dreams.

Live an Inspired Life!

—*Linda Joy*
Inspirational Publisher,
Speaker & Conscious Business Catalyst

PREFACE

I never really thought of myself as a fearful person in my pre-motherhood years. While I have experienced my fair share of fear, I believed back then that I was pretty darn fearless and invincible. When I think about it I was quite brave and bold most of my life on an intellectual level. Mind fear and soul fear are two dramatically different experiences as you know and or will soon discover by reading this book.

Over the years I've faced and conquered many fears but those successes would carry little weight to the fears I faced over the past three years. Growing up fatherless created the fear of being loved. Growing up in a poor single-parent home was the perfect breeding ground for the fear of not having enough money. Growing up overweight set the stage for the fear of not being accepted for who I was on the inside. Growing up in a dysfunctional family provided the opportunity for fear of failure and success. Boy do I have a story to tell. A story that may sound a bit like yours.

There's so much I could tell you about my story yet I will tell you the parts that held the most fear for me. My testimony is simply an example of walking the walk instead of talking the talk. If I'm asking you to be transparent and brutally honest with yourself, well shouldn't I do the same? My closest friends and some family members know bits and pieces of my story but no one, absolutely no one knows the real story. Sound familiar? So I'll share with you a few bitter and sweet moments of my story, this is the first time I ever shared this with anyone outside my inner circle.

I grew up in a single-parent home, poor and raised by a mother who didn't fully know her story. Looking back on my childhood, I realize now that my mother, a woman I admire and love dearly, was broken and bruised. She was living her life on auto-pilot and taking care of us the best way she knew how and with what she had. She was broken because of the villains in her story. She was bruised because of the lies and deceit that infiltrated her mother's story, and her mother's story. You see, I come from a legacy of lies, deceit, pain and struggle. I come from a story where men were scarce and absent. All I remember is women, strong, loving and brave women who shared and passed their stories down to me. I come from a story where men hurt, lied, cheated, abused and disappeared. Men were not to be trusted, counted on and or believed for their word. My story is filled with heroines who did it all by themselves, made it happen no matter what, put their lives on hold for the sake of their children and women who endured hurt, betrayal, disappointment and sometimes even misery. These same women are brilliant loving, resilient, outspoken, wise and compassionate. Despite their past, their story and the unhealthy scripts of their life they found the courage to give love in the best way they knew how. They were fearless women of their time.

My story is that of a fatherless child. My story was full confusion and curiosity as I wondered who my father was. My story had moments of emptiness, fear and unacceptance. How is a young woman suppose to feel about men when her own father denied her, didn't want to have anything to do with her? I'll tell you how. She doesn't trust men, she doesn't believe men and she soon takes on the "I don't need a man mentality" This mentality (life scripts) leads to shame, guilt, callousness and the need to protect one's self. This mentality leads to the urge to overcompensate, overachieve and suit up in rock-solid armor that would shield any pain or discomfort. This mentality leads one to becoming a super-woman, taking on the world, doing it all without needing a man and resenting every moment she wore the cape. This mentality was my mentality, my way of coping with the story of my life. A story filled with many fears my story was.

Our lives are simply a series of moments and stories. Our stories are real and they serve as the script for our lives. Our stories define who we are, what we think, what we believe and how we feel. Just like a written story, your life story is to be written and lived from your vantage point, your reality and your perspective in life. Yet our past stories do not have to be our present or future stories.

Your life may not be going like you imagined it would be. Your life may be empty and missing things, people and events that you long for. Your life may be ordinary and you desire it to be extraordinary. It doesn't matter "how" you describe your life right now. What matters most is how you want it to be, and what you are willing to do to create the life you've dreamed of.

The beautiful thing about it all is that a story can be re-written, revised, and you can create as many alternative endings as you like. You get to choose the characters, the scenes, the moments, the experiences and outcomes. Isn't that fantastic! You see, your life story is simply that a story to be written and lived and you have the choice to re-create the middle, craft the middle and decide how your story will end. Yet you only have the choice if you exercise the power of the pen, your pen.

Everybody has a story, what's yours? The beginning does not determine the end. Your past circumstances do not predict your future. You are the co-creator of your life and you have the power to courageously choose how your story will be lived and create the ending you desire.

Like you, I could not escape fear and it held me captive in many areas of my life for years. Fear caused me to believe I was not good enough, skinny enough, worthy of acceptance and love and fear put a dead bolt double lock on my heart. I never knew who my father was growing up and I had a firm belief that if he could walk out and not love me then anyone and everyone else could too. There were countless moments when fear challenged me, captivated me, sucked the life out of me and had me examining my life from the outside in. I know that I am not alone in these experiences because I have met hundreds of women who once were captive in their own skin, living in fear instead of love.

As you read this book you'll be invited into a very intimate place, my soul, as I share bits and pieces of my story; my story of fear, courage victory and truth. You'll also hear the stores of eleven gracious and transparent women who too found the courage to live their truth by facing and conquering their fears. I cannot put into words my gratitude for their generous contribution to this book and for each story shared I am deeply grateful and thankful.

Introduction

IF YOU ARE ANYTHING LIKE ME, I BET THERE HAVE BEEN TIMES WHEN YOU WISHED YOU HAD A GENIE WHO WOULD GRANT YOU THREE AMAZING WISHES OR MORE. I BET YOU'VE LONGED FOR THE MAGICAL PILL THAT WOULD MAKE EVERYTHING ALL RIGHT. I EVEN BET THAT YOU WISH YOU COULD SNAP YOUR FINGERS AND CREATE THE LIFE YOU DREAM OF. HOW DO I KNOW, BECAUSE I'VE WISHED FOR ALL THOSE THINGS SEVERAL TIMES IN MY LIFE AND BECAME FRUSTRATED AND DISMAYED WHEN THEY DID NOT SHOW UP. I'VE EVEN BEGGED GOD TO PLEASE FIX IT, MAKE IT BETTER, SHOW ME THE WAY AND OR GIVE ME A SIGN.

My wishes were granted but not in ways that I expected and often the answers or wishes were disguised in turmoil, darkness and or despair. I soon realized that the blessing was in the mess and the clarity emerged from chaos. Are you still waiting on a sign, an "aha" moment and or a gold-lantern to land in your lap? You may get the sign and if you are aware you'll experience "aha" moments but unfortunately the genie bottle or gold-lantern is not coming any time soon. This I am certain of yet there is something magical about to happen in your life if you allow it to.

This is a book about more than fear, it is a tribute and celebration to the stories of our lives. It will take you on a magical journey of truth and liberation. The *Art of Fear-Free Living* shares real life stories of women who once lived in fear and now live in love; love of self, love of others and love for life. This book will make you angry, cause tears to well up in your eyes, tickle your heart, challenge your beliefs, stir up your emotions, conjure up a few chuckles and hopefully be a big, loud alarm clock to wake up your soul and cause you to start running towards your dreams. My intention is that you run with faith, courage and fearlessness to do more than chase your dreams but live them bold and brave. I even imagine if you really apply the strategies offered in this book you will become frustrated and maybe even a little more afraid. This will be a "good fear" experience because for once in your life you will realize that fear can be the fuel to fire you up and ignite the desires of your heart.

I speak to you with candid compassion in this book. I keep it real yet am mindful that your life is your life and how you live it is your choice. As a Fear-Free Living Expert it's my calling to inspire and empower you wake up the Geni(us) within; that all-knowing, wise, confident, resilient SHero who is begging to be released. One of the main intentions for writing this book is to inspire you to seek, discover, accept, embrace, speak and live your truth. The truth of your story, the truth of who you are, the truth about your fears, the truth about your dreams and the truth about who you desire to become and how you desire to show up in the world. They don't say "the truth will set you free" just for the fun of it. There is healing, transformational power in the truth. There is liberation and joyful release in the truth. I hope you find the courage to live your truth. In fact, I am holding space for you to stand brave in your truth right now.

Since the beginning of time human beings have sought the truth and went above and beyond their perceived capabilities to discover it. I've always been a curious woman; a woman on a relentless quest of the truth, my truth. Instead of making New Year's resolutions for 2011, I decided to choose one word that would be the intention for the rest of my life. I chose the word truth. In truth there is fear. In truth there is worry, doubt and anxiety. Yes, the truth and seeking it can be an exhausting and scary. Yet there is something greater, more profound and enlightening in discovering the truth. In truth there is liberation, clarity, and direction. Once you clear out the fogginess of the fear of the truth the path to who we are to become is opened. The chapters' once lingering open can be closed. The heaviness of the unknowing is lifted. In seeking, discovering and knowing the truth we are set free! Although we may experience some pain or discomfort in seeking the truth, once it's revealed to us we can let go, embrace our reality and know that simply in seeking the truth we are brave.

My hope for you is that you begin your journey of truth no matter what it is. It may feel scary and you may be afraid but BE COURAGEOUS IN THE MIDST OF FEAR. Every step towards fear decreases its power. Every courageous action makes you more fearless. When you are afraid give your energy to this question "what do I need to conquer this fear" instead of becoming paralyzed by the fear. The more resources and support you have as you face your fears increases the courage you'll have to be a fearless champion.

Life is one big story and the world is creating the novel of humanity in every moment. Every single thought we have, feeling we express or repress, and every action we take or do not take is creating the story of our lives. We are either creating our stories through the power of our love pen or our fear pen. When we author our stories in fear we deny our story to be filled with happiness, joy, satisfaction and a zest for life. Our fear pen writes in the shadows and doesn't allow the light in our lives to shine though. Our fear pen really never allows us to write a new chapter in our lives because it only knows how to write and re-write the horror, pain and suffering of the past. If the fear pen is able to create a new chapter it fills the pages with the same old drama, misery, self-sabotaging recollections of the bad and the ugly and rarely the good. The fear pen keeps you wallowing in the past, holding grudges, doubting yourself and stifling your dreams.

Now our love pen, that's a whole new literary Geni(us). It has a power of its own and creates words of lyrical delight on the white pages of our lives. The love pen writes from a place of forgiveness, acceptance and gratitude for all that is good and bad in our lives. The love pen holds no grudges, it is free from the captivity of the past bondage in our lives. The love pen knows that what happened to us is not who we are rather events that happened in our lives. The love pen is brave, courageous and seeks to share the authenticity of who we are deep in our souls. The story of our lives written with the love pen speaks the truth, embraces every part of who we are, honors our experiences and allows us to celebrate the light in all situations.

Your pen comes in the form of the thoughts you think, the actions you take and the words you speak. The life you live is the result of the story you tell yourself, others and the stories that live in your heart. If you are living in fear you will think, speak, feel and behave fearfully. Fear shows up as doubt, worry, anxiety, panic, shame, guilt, procrastination, denial, immobilization and a long list of other things that keep you captive within your own skin. When you live in love it shows up as confidence, trust, acceptance, faith, action, movement and ultimately knowing all may not be perfect but all is well.

Creating your life with your love pen takes more work and of course courage but the journey and the ending is so much more fulfilling. The choice is yours. Live and create in fear or live and create in love; it's that simple. In every second of your life you are creating not only your story but the legacy you'll leave for your children and their children. What story do you want BE, LIVE, CREATE and leave behind? If you want to live different, better, bigger, more joyful then stop telling the sob stories, the pity stories, the "I live in the past" stories and all the other stories that defeat your greatness, dim your light and silence your SHero. Take back your power today and start telling stories of love, courage, victory, success and see how your life will dramatically change. Every time you tell a negative story of the past whether consciously or subconsciously you plant the negative seed deeper into your soul. Every negative seed festers and grows into a weed garden flourishing with regret, resentment, frustration and apathy. When you begin to tell stories of truth, stories of courage and stories of accomplishment the weeds die off and seedlings of purpose, passion and pleasure begin to take root. As you tell these stories consistently the seeds bloom into hope, faith, strength, courage and resiliency. These kinds of stories uplift, inspire, empower and equip you with the tools you need to live a fearlessly delicious life.

I hope you choose to pick up a new, powerful pen today. The pen of love and create the life you dream of; a life that fulfills you, a life that makes you and your family proud, a life that you crave, anticipate and love. In this moment, you now have an unlimited stack of clear paper to re-write your story. Before you in your mind, heart and soul you have two pens; the love pen and the fear pen. Which one will you pick up today? Take out your first sheet of paper, pick up your love pen and let your courage voice speak the words to be written in the book of your life. There's a Genie eager to be released; a wise Genie who knows what you need, desire and want in your life. The Genie you've been waiting for has been with you all along. Prepare yourself for an amazing and enlightening soul adventure; a magical moment where you courageously pop the top on your Genie bottle and release her: your SHero, your Geni(us). Be fearless and may God be with you on your journey.

It's time to master your mind and master
The Art of Fear-Free Living.

ONE

KEEPING IT REAL: THE TRUTH ABOUT FEAR

*I*S FEAR SUCKING THE LIFE OUT OF YOU AND STEALING YOUR DREAMS? YOU JUST MIGHT BE LIVING IN FEAR IF YOU ARE STRESSED, CONFUSED, FRUSTRATED, DOUBTFUL, WORRYING, ANGRY AND PROCRASTINATING IN YOUR LIFE. THAT CAN ALL END WHEN YOU ARE READY TO GET OUT OF YOUR SELF-CREATED MISERY AND STOP WALLOWING IN SELF-PITY AND FEARFULNESS. FEAR IS A FUTURE STATE OF MIND AND EMOTION. THAT'S RIGHT IT HASN'T HAPPENED YET.

When you master *The Art of Fear-Free Living* you learn how to embrace and maximize the power of NOW. You cannot create in chaos, you cannot vividly dream in mental conflict, you can not manifest in a fearful mindset. Mastering *The Art of Fear Free Living* gives you the power to believe it, dream it, create it and live it—your dream life!

I hope you weren't too surprised by the opening to this chapter. Simply put, you cannot change anything unless you acknowledge it first. You'll see that I use a candid and compassionate approach to writing, teaching and speaking and I do it all in love and truth. It's time for you to get real about your life if you expect to experience real results. Now that we've got that out of the way, let's get down to creating some magic. You are reading this book because you are experiencing fear in your life and or you desire to be more courageous. If you are dedicated and committed to living a fearless life the one thing you must do is be honest with yourself, period. A courageous, fear-free life is not for the faint of heart.

You only have one life to live and there will be moments when you put your love gloves on, climb into the ring of life and fight like it's the last fight of your life. There will be moments when the people you love will try to keep you confined to their expectations of how you should live your life and you'll need to be courageous enough to say "this is my life and I am going to live it on my own terms." There will be moments when you don't know where the next step will take you but you will boldly put one foot in front of the other and step into your greatness. There will be moments when you want to give up because it becomes too hard and you will summon the champion within. There will be moments when you attempt to talk yourself out of your blessing and destiny and you will have to tell that inner critic to shut up and take a back seat. Oh yes, all of these moments will occur during your journey of fearless living throughout your life so choose now to awaken your Geni(us) and arm her with the secret weapon of love. Love conquers all and love and fear cannot exist in the same space. There is only one choice, continue to live in fear or choose love as your path to courage and fearless living.

I want you to know that when you choose to live fearless things will change. The greatest change will occur within you but it's fair to inform you your circle of friends will change as well. People will begin to see you differently and potentially

respond negatively to your brave transformation. You'll
especially see this shift if you have friends who are settling
for the status quo; those living in mediocrity and miserably
wallowing in a fear pool of nagging, complaining and
blaming other people for the content of their lives. When
you say yes to your life and summon your inner Geni(us)
these folks will feel abandoned and threatened. They will say
"you've changed" and may even directly and or indirectly
cut you off and cut you out of their lives. I believe it's fair
to warn you that some of your closest friends and dearest
family members will openly or silently attempt to sabotage
your success. My hope for you is that the people you love
and care about will honor your choice and support you and
or go on the journey with you. I know for sure that some
will and some won't; are you ready for this? The choice to
live fearlessly has risks, but don't worry, everything you
need you already have within you and if you need more it's
in this book.

Read Carla's story and see how she handled this as it
happened in her life.

FEAR DREW A LINE THAT SHUT ME OUT, LOVE DREW A CIRCLE THAT TOOK ME IN

Dr. Carla Goddard's Story

I had been friends with a core group for years. They were my network, the foundation I depended on when life happens, and the ones I allowed into my private world. They were the ones I called when I just had to share the funny incident at the store or the tears when someone I loved crossed from this world. We all have that inner circle. We think that it will be forever. It was our friendship that bonded us. As I was traversing this journey, something happened. Something changed. It was me. I looked up in the sky one afternoon feeling the rays of the sun and life was good. In that moment, as I felt the warmth of the sun, I had a knowing of where I was going on this path. I had a knowing of who I was—I was no longer becoming. I knew. My inner being knew.

As the fullness of this knowing settled in, so did something else. It was called fear. Fear that as I stepped into my knowing the bonds in that inner circle would be broken. I was changing. My path was changing. So too, came the realization, would my inner circle. Many thoughts consumed me and made me pause before taking another step. The circle of friends was based upon the old path of becoming, the old thoughts of wondering and the old belief patterns of self-doubt. With this new found knowing, I wondered if things would still be the same.

Thoughts of "could I do this on my own", "are losing these bonds worth it", and I thought "maybe I should just stay the course and hang onto what seems real" because my 'friends' were constant in my conscious. Fear can paralyze. It can steal a dream. It can cause a stagnation that puts out fires. As I struggled with this fear and the thoughts that emerged, I knew I had to make a choice. The choice was to live authentically within my knowing or stifle my dreams, my truth. I shared my excitement and new knowing with these friends. I shared my fire and passion. I shared my visions and dreams. I shared my new path. Wouldn't they then want to share in them too? Wouldn't they hear my passion and find their own? Wouldn't we be on this new exciting journey together? The friends in this inner circle were happy with their lives. They did not wish to change and evolve their own paths. I was finding that letting go of the ties that bound us was one of those processes that was so difficult and painful. Lines were drawn.

Suddenly I was the outsider. I was perceived as the one that was excluded and full of farfetched dreams. I was the one who was thought of as not being available for the quick phone calls and coffee at the drop of a hat. I was the one who was told I was being self-centered and creating drama as I ignored my 'friends'. The fears returned. Letting go of this circle, the knowing burning deep within, remaining focused on my vision, something amazing happened. The circle grew. This tiny limited circle I had created around me was stifling my ability to follow my path. Letting go actually spurred a growth of the circle tenfold. Those around me suddenly were ones who knew too, they had dreams, they had visions, and they were following them.

I was still grieving the loss of the small network, when one in this large circle whispered to me "stop regretting and start living." I have memories of the funny moments, the happy moments, and all the moments in between. Memories are in the past and they are not my vision of the future. As I let go more and more, the circle got larger and larger. Love encompassed me.

The soul connection is deeper with each person in this ever expanding circle. The fear never eliminated, yet the courage to follow the knowing transformed the grief and struggle into the most amazing circle of love I have today. Discovering your knowing, your authentic path is an amazing gift. To experience the deep knowing within allows you the freedom to truly create your desired reality. It is a deep fire. It is that knowing that provides the courage and trust necessary to let go of what was. They say courage is not the absence of fear, but doing in spite of fear. I have had some amazing miracles happen as a result of living my authentic path. There have been many times that fear has crept in. I have found that courage and trust has come from the most unexpected places. Listen to the voice within and ask for strength to forge ahead. Ask for direction. Ask for courage. Ask for a friend that knows too. There has never been a single experience where I have asked, and it has not been given. Sometimes I am unable see the gift being given until after it is already opened.

Trusting in this very moment that it will unfold to share with you exactly what you need to know is the true gift—it is then that the external event can transform into inner knowing.

—*Dr. Carla Goddard, Sacred Soul Shaman*
www.ashiramedicinewoman.blogspot.com

I applaud Carla for taking the risks, stepping out on faith and trusting her knowing as she let go of the people who were settling for less, weighing down her dreams and dimming her light. What I appreciate the most about Carla's story is she took steps in the dark not knowing where each step would take her. Carla listened to her Geni(us), that divine voice inside that never leads you astray

We didn't share this story to scare you and add more fear to your life but to prepare you for the potential detours, pot holes and roadblocks you are sure to experience when you begin the journey of mastering *The Art of Fear-Free Living*. It's the nature of the beast, it's part of life and you cannot control how other people respond to your courageous act of self-love. The only thing you can control is how you respond to their re-action. Remember, this is your life and you are now in the driver's seat and in control to co-create the life you dream of.

The truth about fear is that it will always be a part of your life. The truth about fear is that it is a most often a future state of mind. The truth about fear is that the best weapon against it is love. The truth about fear is that it is powerful beyond measure. The final truth about fear is that love of yourself, love of life, love for other people and love for the world can diminish the power of fear and afford you more peace, joy, ease and grace in your life. The truth about you is that you can choose to be fearless by living in the now moment, you can choose to love and accept who you are in your core and you can choose love when fear steps in.

It's time for you to break free from the tightly woven fibers of fear and emerge into the world confident, free and liberated. As you continue on this journey of living fearless always know that you have three powerful companions. When you feel afraid put your hand on your heart and summons and awakens your Geni(us), activate your courage compass and call forth your champion. You'll learn more about these three power choices as you read further. Keep taking steps in the dark and know Carla and I are with you and we send you love and light. Trust yourself because you are the Geni(us) so strap on your boxing gloves of love and get ready! Get ready to be challenged, stretched, and expanded because it's your time to break free. It's your moment soar above and beyond your fears.

*"You must want to fly so much
that you are willing to give up being a caterpillar."*

—*Anonymous*

TWO

FEAROLOGY:

Understanding the Language, Power and Manifestation of Fear

*T*HE AMOUNT OF FEAR YOU LIVE IN IS THE RESULT OF YOUR THOUGHTS, BELIEFS, FEELINGS AND ACTIONS. WE ALL WERE BORN WITH A SELF-CRITIC WHICH SERVES ONE PURPOSE, TO SOMETIMES KEEP US SAFE AND KEEP US STUCK.

Now you may be wondering why we would be born with something that keeps us stuck and how in the world can it keep us safe at the same time. Well, for example, if you were about to walk in the middle of traffic the self-critic would say "no, don't do that you could get hurt or die." Thus the critic is working at its best to keep you safe. That same critic or voice can also keep you stuck by whispering self-defeating thoughts into your spirit such as, "becoming famous is scary and dangerous and when you do people will treat you differently." This message subconsciously keeps you from elevating to your highest self and reaching for your big dreams of success thus keeping you stuck in settling for small dreams of success.

When your self-critic works to hold you back from fully living your life the outcome is you are stuck; stuck in limiting beliefs, negative mental tapes and simply settling for what is rather than what can be.

They key is to learn how to discern the difference between when the critic is keeping you safe versus attempting to keep you stuck. That power is within you and it has always been there. You may have been looking for the power outside of yourself in the past but today and from this day forth, know that it is and will always be within you. Now just because it is there doesn't mean it will be easy to execute it in every situation. Some life circumstances and events will create such chaos and confusion that you will have to work a little harder to hear the voice of liberation and freedom. I know you can do that especially when you learn what your language of fear speaks like.

We were all uniquely created and we are wired differently based upon many factors to include genetics, experiences and our environment. These factors help determine how we think, how we perceive the world in which we live and how we respond to our environments, people, places and events. I have no intention of defining that language for you yet I encourage you to define it, understand it and learn how it shows up and manifests in your life. I will share with you how fear speaks to me and how its voice either keeps me safe or attempts to keep me stuck.

MY FATHER STORY

Catrice Jackson's story

On February 4, 2011 I did a DNA paternity test with my alleged father. He was the only man I'd ever known to be my father. I'd waited 41 years to know this truth. I thought about discovering the truth several times in my life but didn't have the courage to face the truth. I was afraid. I was afraid not to necessarily know but more afraid of what would happen to the relationship I had with my mother if he was not. After finding my birth certificate in January 2011 (it took 41 years) another truth milestone, I discovered two more truths. I had lived most of my life as a Johnson (before marriage) but legally I was someone else. Last November I celebrated my birthday on the 17th yet discovered this year I was born on the 18th. Wow! The truth is something else but without knowing it we will always remain in the "unknowing" of life. I'm not angry, I don't blame anyone and besides aren't those just numbers and dates? They don't define who I am or determine the value that I bring to the world.

Back to my father story. On February 10, 2011 I found out that there is a 0% chance that "he" my alleged father could be my father and he is not my father. This story of truth is bittersweet. It's bitter because I would have liked for this part of the journey to end here. The sweet part is that there is one more potential father option to be explored. I may just discover in this journey of truth that my best friend of 20+ years, may be in fact my 1st cousin. If this is true, I've been with my family all along and that is deliciously sweet. God works in mysterious ways and he knows what we need all the time.

17

One thing is 100% the truth...I've never been fatherless, the greatest father any woman could have is our heavenly father who loved me before I was conceived, cared for me as I grew and loved me unconditionally no matter what. Thank you father God, I love you!

I had many opportunities to find out who my father was or at least to rule out whether this man was my father. Fear kept me from seeking, discovering and experiencing the truth. My inner critic often said "if he is your father, what if he doesn't want to have a relationship with you, if he is your father what if his family does not accept you and if he isn't your father, you know that's going to damage the relationship you have with your mother." Sometimes my critic spoke loudly and other times it showed up as a whisper.

—Catrice Jackson

I now know the language, pitch and tone of my inner critic and have learned how to silence it. Ultimately, the voice of fear lives and thrives in your mind. When you allow your thoughts to become consumed by fear, the ripple effect of fear begins to penetrate your spirit and can show its ugly face in your physical body. Fear's favorite conversation always shows up the same. It speaks of doubt, worry, lack, danger, procrastination, envy, mistrust and a long list of other time-wasting energy. Fear has several favorite statements such as "I can't, I don't have time, it will never work, I don't have enough money, what will people think of me and you guessed it, the list is endless. If you are living in fear I guarantee that your dreams will go unfulfilled, your relationships will not be satisfying, you'll never have enough money and you will allow the opinions of others to determine the direction, content and quality of your life. By now you should have a good idea of how powerful fear is by what you've read thus far and by what you are currently experiencing in your life.

Fear's power is elusive, sneaky and at times abstract. At the source of dis(ease) within the human spirit lies fear; brooding, lingering, holding on to the smallest fiber of your being and waiting for the opportunity to sabotage your success, steal your dreams and make life miserable. Fear is the quicksand that many wallow in, fight to get out of yet often succumb to the lethal effects of its power. Fear comes in many shapes, sizes and flavors and if you are not living awakened it will captivate your ability to live free and fulfilled. Many fears are obvious like fear of failure, fear of success and or fear of leaving an unhealthy relationship. Yet other fears are not so obvious such as fear of money, fear of exposure and or fear of your personal power. What is clear; is fear keeps you in a state of settling.

Whether your fear is obvious or not if you are living in fear you tend to settle for less, settle for mediocrity, and or settle for an unfulfilled life. If you have dreams yet are not taking the steps to bring them to life, you are settling. If you would love to travel but can't seem to get to the places you desire, you are settling. If you want to be in a healthy, loving relationship yet remain alone, you are settling. If you are watching your friends excel and enjoy their lives yet you accept the status quo in your life, of course, you are settling. You'll hear me say this one thing over and over again, "you have the power within you to choose to live in fear or be courageous and face your fears. It's that simple, period. Once you realize these are your only two options you'll soon discover that only you can choose the option that best suits you. I offer you in the next several chapters the choice and the tools to master *The Art of Fear-Free Living*, a choice that will empower you to:

- Gain more clarity, focus and direction.
- Worry less and take inspired action.
- Face challenges instead of avoiding them.
- Turn your pain into powerful possibilities.
- Transition from dreading life to living and loving life.
- Quiet the inner critic and wake up your champion.
- Learn how to say no to misery and yes to what brings you joy.
- Take your dream off the shelf and bring it to life.
- Live in love versus wallowing in fear.

Mastering *The Art of Fear-Free Living* requires you to wake up, bring your fears to the surface, examine them, step towards them and face them with full intention, faith and belief. You must believe that you possess the power within to create and live life more courageously. There is a Geni(us) sleeping inside of you waiting on you to gently stroke your heart and wake it up. There is a Geni(us) inside of you begging to come alive and help you align and activate your life. There is a Geni(us) inside of you ready to be your guide as you begin a new journey into unknown territory. That Geni(us) is your intuition, your soul's voice, your courage compass... your champion! Your inner champion is cheering you on right now can you hear her or are you listening to the inner critic?

This is a divine moment to let go of your old ways of doing and being in life. Everything you need you already have so trust yourself, trust your wisdom, trust your abilities and trust that you and only you know what you need, want and desire in your life. When you consistently live in an awakened and intentional state of consciousness "the knowing within" will guide you towards your next steps and you do "it" afraid in faith. It's time for you leave this place of mediocrity, begin your journey and awaken your Geni(us). Leaving can be hard but remember you have two choices, leave and be liberated or stay and be swallowed up by fear. Amy left and so can you when you are ready and the time is right. Whatever you need to leave behind let your champion and your Geni(us) be your guide.

LEAVING

Amy O'Brien's Story

Boxes were stacked in the foyer and spilling over into the living room. I sat teary-eyed on the sofa after spending two days with my soon-to-be-ex boyfriend, packing all of my things in preparation for the move, and pretty much crying the entire time. I bought a home sixty miles south for my two sons and I, and Joe wasn't invited. The boys were spending the weekend with their father, and my brother was about to arrive with the moving truck.

The crying isn't what you think. We'd only lived together for about a year and a half, and the last half felt like death by a thousand paper cuts. My friend Stephanie would listen as I gave her a complete recount of what had happened the night before as we commuted into the city on the train each morning:

"Joe asked me to go to the LL Bean Outlet with him in New Hampshire yesterday, and he spent the entire one-hour drive home talking to his friend on his cell phone."

"Joe thinks I should do all of his laundry because I'm already doing so much with the kids that he thinks one or two more shouldn't be a big deal to me."

"He constantly hovers over me when I'm at the stove, telling me what his mother would think of the way I cook. Yet he doesn't seem to have any trouble eating what I make. He's also decided that he will only help with the dishes if/when he feels like it."

"Joe said that given my situation (I have kids) I should feel lucky just to have a guy around."

The man I once saw as a good friend and lover turned into a person I couldn't stand. Still, I hadn't spent that much time alone after my divorce three years before. I was moving to a town where I knew no one, and leaving a community I'd grown to love in the short period of time I spent there. I worried about how my children would adjust to a new school.

Searching for a new home had practically become a second occupation. In six months I'd gone to more than one hundred open houses in fifteen different communities, and spent hours looking on-line to see what was available. At that time, I was teaching yoga and I'd developed a spiritual practice that involved studying my dreams and intuition. The tough thing about intuition is that it doesn't always tell you what you want to hear. While my gurgling stomach, urge to flee, and symbolic dreams may have been giving me clear signs that said, "Get away from him, he isn't right for you," the logistics involved caused me to question it and try to invalidate it. No matter how much I tried to pretend everything would work out, my gut would have none of it.

My search seemed fruitless as nothing in my price range felt right. One night, before I allowed myself to drift off to sleep, I prayed for God's help. I dreamed I was driving and came upon a sign—"Wrentham" with an arrow pointing south. I awoke thinking, "Wrentham? What's in Wrentham?" The only time I'd ever been to Wrentham, Massachusetts was when my friend Pam took me to the Outlets to buy new clothes after my divorce—a little retail therapy. Curious, I checked realtor.com and found a townhouse that met my criteria, except for the fact that it wasn't a single family home, so I ignored the sign, and kept looking.

Two months later, Joe grabbed my seven-year-old son by the throat and forced him out the kitchen door. He stopped short of hurting him, then denied he did anything wrong after I warned him never to lay a hand on my child ever again. His behavior was starting to escalate, and I knew we needed to go. I again prayed for a sign telling me where. A few nights later, I dreamed I was looking at a beige house. On its For Sale sign was a picture of a bright red cardinal with trees in the background. I strained to see the words—Woodland or Forest, I can't remember.

As I waited for my computer to boot up, I told myself to check that townhouse again, and if the condo association's name... I was stunned when the words "Forest Park" stared back at me. I picked up the phone and dialed Jeannette, the listing agent.

That afternoon, on a dreary day in February, I made the trek south, all the while wondering if I was crazy to be listening to a dream. Then again, I thought, don't all good things start with a dream? Within seconds of walking through the front door, I knew. This was our new home. I'd found it. Two months later I was at the court house, signing the closing papers.

Leaving Joe was tough. Even though I knew he wasn't right for me, and in spite of his narcissistic and bullyish ways, there were still those moments of laughter and conversation—the companionship of another adult I so miss as a single mother. I cried for the end of my marriage and the dream of an intact family. I cried over the loss of a friend and lover whose original charm had turned toxic. I cried over lost friendships and the familiarity of not only this home, but the marriage home I'd sold. I cried out of fear of the unknown. I continued to cry for days as I unpacked boxes, and slept each night on the sofa until my new bed arrived. I wondered if I made a huge mistake, while at the same time, believing I made the right decision.

A week later, I poured myself a cup of coffee, walked over to my back door, and looked out at the state forest behind our home. When a bright red cardinal landed in a tree, an overwhelming sense of peace flooded my body, as though someone had hugged me from the inside out. It was at that moment that my crying stopped, and I started smiling again. I had honored my intuition. I did what was right for my family. My boys made a new best friend and liked their new school. Finally, I had inner peace, and peace within my home.

The bright red cardinal's mate laid eggs in the cedars, and it wasn't until the baby flew off weeks later that the birds stopped coming. Now, whenever I see a cardinal, I'm reminded not to be afraid. Everything will work out. All I have to do is have faith, and listen.

—*Amy Beth O'Brien*
Author of *Stuck with Mr. Wrong?*
Ten Steps to Starring in your own Life Story.
http://www.amybethobrien.com

Have you had dreams like Amy but been ignoring them? Does your gut tell you get out, walk away, let go or leave (a job, relationship, home, community or situation)? Are you listening to your inner critic who is trying to trick you into staying stuck? I love Amy's story because she shares several dilemmas that many women face and how we tend to put others needs before our own; how we deny the brilliant woman within. Amy's story perfectly illustrates something very familiar to women just like me and you; we'd rather sacrifice our hopes, dreams and aspirations rather than create chaos and discomfort for our children. But know this, dear one, staying hurts everyone involved. I hope Amy's story inspires you to not wait for potential danger or until you are sick and tired of being sick and tire. I hope her story validates your brilliance and empowers you to create the internal and external peace and knowing you long for. In that moment in time Amy knew for sure where she was and where she needed to be. Now it's your turn. You can do it. Amy is an ordinary woman with extraordinary personal power just like me and you!

Before you begin your new journey you must assess where you are in this moment so you know exactly where you want to be. Remember, you cannot change what you do not acknowledge, and it's more difficult to get to your destination if you don't know your starting point. Mastering *The Art of Fear-Free Living* is a journey of honesty, courage and transparency. Be completely honest in your answers, be courageous enough to tell the truth about where you are and don't be afraid to look deep within as you complete the Pre-Fear Assessment.

This assessment was not created to judge you but to give you a glimpse into the amount of fear you may be living in. There are no right or wrong answers and the rating scale was not created to shock or scare you. Simply use the rating scale to determine the level of fear or the intensity of fear you may be experiencing at this moment in time. Do not rush through the assessment just to continue reading. In fact, I suggest that you do not read the next chapter until you have completed the assessment. So take some time, find a quiet place and allow yourself to be completely vulnerable and honest as you take the assessment. After completing it, try to digest what you see in black and white and think about how fear is specifically captivating your life. Then take a deep breath and say "I am fearless," then begin reading the next chapter.

"You gain strength, courage and confidence by every experience in which you really stop to look fear in the face. You must do the thing, which you think you cannot do."

—*Eleanor Roosevelt*

Fear Pre-Assessment

Please complete this assessment before reading further.

Use this scale (1-10) to rate your level of fear about the following issues.

Date of Assessment _____   Time _____

10=Extreme Fear 8=Significant Fear 5=Moderate Fear
1= Very Little Fear 0= None

___I worry about not having enough money to pay my bills

___I worry that I won't achieve my goals.

___I worry about people not supporting my dream.

___I worry that something bad is going to happen to me.

___I'm concerned that I may not have what it takes to be successful.

___I fear that others will talk about me if I take steps forward.

___I am afraid to fail.

___I fear that I am not good enough or that I don't deserve good things.

___I'm fear that my intimate relationship will not last.

___I'm afraid to dream.

___I am afraid I will lose my close relationships if I become successful.

___I fear success.

___I am afraid to die.

___I fear that I will lose my job.

___I am afraid to take risks.

___I am afraid my past will always haunt me.

___I am afraid to make mistakes.

___I fear the economic climate will keep me from having what I want.

___I fear that people are trying to undermine my success.

___I fear that my health will get worse.

___I'm afraid to quit my job and begin a career.

___I'm afraid to leave my relationship.

___I fear the unknown.

___I fear that God won't bless my life.

___I am afraid of my own power.

___I am afraid of just about everything.

*List your score here: _____

"The question isn't who is going to let me, it's who is going to stop me."

—*Ayn Rand*

THREE
WAKE UP
YOUR FEAR GIANTS

C ONGRATULATIONS ON COMPLETING THE FEAR PRE-ASSESSMENT! HOW DOES IT FEEL RIGHT NOW IN THIS MOMENT TO KNOW HOW MUCH FEAR YOU ARE LIVING IN OR BETTER YET HOW COURAGEOUS YOU ARE? MY HOPE IS THAT YOU WERE HONEST IN YOUR ASSESSMENT BECAUSE IF YOU WEREN'T YOU ARE SIMPLY SETTING YOURSELF UP FOR FAILURE. IF YOU DID NOT HONESTLY RESPOND TO THE QUESTIONS, PLEASE GO BACK AND DO THE ASSESSMENT AGAIN. YOU'LL DO THIS SAME ASSESSMENT UPON THE COMPLETION OF THE BOOK TO MEASURE YOUR FEARLESS LIVING SUCCESS.

The first step in mastering *The Art of Fear-Free Living* is to acknowledge your fears, bring them to the surface and embrace them. This is one of the most courageous steps of the process and must be done with complete honesty. Your fears have been giants in your life for some time now and just as you must wake up your Geni(us) you too must awaken those fear giants. This may be the most difficult part of the journey so get ready to dig deep and be gentle and patient with yourself. In this chapter you'll bring your fears to the surface to determine where you are and then create a vision for where you want to be and how you will live more fearlessly. You can choose to lie to yourself and leave some fears on the back burner or you can be courageously honest and bring all of them to the surface.

I want you to think deeply about your life. I want you to step outside of yourself for a moment and try to see yourself as if you were watching your life on a hidden camera. I want you to get creative and literally see captions over your head as you move through your life. I want you to visualize the random, persistent and or consistent thoughts that float around in your head. I want you to see yourself either moving forward or standing still and why you are taking action or procrastinating. I want you to notice everything you do or fail to do and why. After watching yourself sit quietly for a moment and pay attention to the fears that rise up in your belly. As you wait for them to appear, because they will indeed, think about the following questions. Then I want to you write down your top five fears, how they show up in your life whether they are real or F.E.A.R (false evidence appearing real).

Life Reflection Questions

1. When I show up in the world in any circumstance and with anyone am I truly my authentic self?

2. Do I live each day with intention and focus on living the life that I dream of?

3. What am I resisting, avoiding or talking myself out of?

4. Who in my life is lifting me up or bringing me down?

5. At what moments, which circumstances and with whom am I most afraid?

Keep asking yourself these questions and freely write down whatever comes to mind. Pay attention to how you are feeling as you think of these questions and the responses. Notice whether you experience tension, anxiety, peace or joy. The questions and or responses that create the most discomfort are an indication you are near the source of your fears. Do not resist the feelings you are experiencing. This is a very powerful and pivotal moment in the journey. If you do this correctly you will reveal some truths about what you fear, why you fear it and who may be contributing to your fears. In the space below now list your top five fears, how they show up in your life and how they are keeping your Geni(us) captive.

My Top Five Fears

Fear #1

Fear #2

Fear #3

Fear #4

Fear #5

Bringing your fears to the surface can be uncomfortable. I want you to be patient, loving and gentle with yourself as you take each step in this journey. Trust that you know what you need, when you need it and exactly how it needs to show up in your life. As you reflect upon your top five fears, what comes up for you? What are you thinking and feeling in this moment? My hope is that you feel a sense of relief a sense of liberation. It's important for you to now examine those fears at an even deeper level. As human beings, we have the tendency to catastrophize our fears, blow them up bigger than what they really are and create a lot of mental chaos. So the next step is to test out the theory of F.E.A.R (false evidence appearing real). Please take some time to do the next exercise.

You will need five sheets of paper and a whole lot of honesty to do this exercise. On each sheet of paper write one of your top five fears on the top of the paper and then write the following statement on one side of the paper; "what is the worst that could happen if I face this fear." On the other side of each sheet of paper write this statement; "what is the worst that could happen if I do not face this fear." When you write about the worst that could happen I want you to go all out and speak truthfully about what "could" happen in either scenario. This is your only chance to blow your fears out of proportion because once you finish this exercise it's time to get real, honest and very intentional about conquering those fears.

Now that you've completed this exercise you should have a very clear perspective on what your top five fears are, how they show up in your life, how they affect your thoughts, feelings and action and how real or ridiculous they are. Quite often when I have my coaching clients participate in this exercise, they clearly see that they have blown their fears up unnecessarily and that they have more to lose by not facing their fears than they do by facing them. I hope this is what you've just experienced. As I stated earlier, fear is a state of mind. Fear lives and thrives in our minds and it is in your mind that you face and conquer it.

Before you begin to create the fearless vision for your life, I want to take these newly revealed fears to a deeper level of understanding. Fear is at the root of all of your negative or discomforting feelings. Where there is worry there is fear. Where there is doubt there is fear. Take just a minute and think about the things or people you are worrying about and or doubting including yourself.

When you experience "good" or positive feelings they are an expression of love. When you experience "bad" or negative feelings they are bubbling up from a place of fear. An essential part of the journey to mastering *The Art of Fear-Free Living* and awakening your Geni(us) is your ability to identify your feelings, feel them, process them and then take an intentional action. I challenge you to explore the questions below now and as you continue to read this book and beyond.

Reflective Feeling Questions

When I am worried,
I am fearing_____

When I am sad,
I am fearing_____

When I am doubtful,
I am fearing _____

When I am angry,
I am fearing _____

When I am lonely,
I am fearing _____

When I am jealous,
I am fearing _____

When I am anxious,
I am fearing _____

When I am confused,
I am fearing _____

To continue going deeper into your fears I want you to start paying attention to your feelings. Your feelings are the result of your thoughts and if you can become more aware of what you are feeling you will be able to trace those feelings back to a particular thought or set of thinking patterns. Once you identify the thoughts; the language of the inner critic, you then have the power to create and choose new thoughts and language.

Give yourself a pat on the back you have done some brave and brilliant work towards Mastering *The Art of Fear-Free Living*. I applaud your courageous efforts and know that you are on your way to living more fearless with each step you take. By now you have defined fear, understand its language and power, how it manifests in your life, your top five fears and what your life will be like if you do or do not face your fears. If you honestly look back on the exercises and your responses you should see a theme and most importantly that one BIG fear that keeps your Geni(us) bottled up. If you have not yet identified it, don't worry you will as you continue on your fearless journey. One of the biggest fears you will learn to conquer in this book is the fear of the unknown. Life will always serve you up a big dose of the unknown and often times on a pretty silver platter, the good news is that you will be empowered to pick up your silver spoon and eat it up with confidence and courage by the time you finish this book and apply the fearless living strategies to your life every day. Take a journey into Angela's story and see how she embraced the uncomfortableness, beauty and power in the unknown.

FEAR OF THE UNKNOWN

Angela's Schaefer's Story

I lived in a state of anxiety for many years. When I realized what was at the core of the anxiety, not how I had developed an anxiety disorder, things finally changed. The anxiety I woke up and went to sleep with each night was based on feelings of the unknown. I never knew what the next day would hold. I did not know what tragedies or challenges I would face.

I had endured a life, since childhood, of neglect, poverty and abuse in some form or another. I suffered a traumatic childhood injury that lead to years of medical care. When I thought it was safe, that nothing else could go wrong or happen to me, the inevitable would happen. It was impossible for a long span of time to occur between one challenge to the next.

Realizing that the unknown of many things in my life were creating a lack of peace, joy and gratitude I knew something had to change. I was tired physically and emotionally from years of anxiety taking its toll on me. The fear of the unknown problems that each day could bring was gripping and paralyzing. Ongoing physical ailments and emotional distress was a way of life for me.

I started the change by acknowledging the blessings in my life and to have an attitude of gratitude. I had to learn what I could control and not control in my life. I needed to remember, each new day, that all that had already happened was over and unchangeable. I realized that there were very few things I had control over. When I was realistic it came down to two things; how I reacted to people and circumstances and how I chose to perceive things and people around me. Everything else was simply life happening around me and my attitude towards it could help or hinder me.

Committing myself to change, to let go of the fear of the unknown, was a process. Letting go of the routine thoughts, I had for over thirty years, of all the things that could go wrong required breaking an old and deeply instilled habit. When I reached the age of thirty six years I had finally succeeded, just in time to face the unknown of cancer. I had learned from a part of my story, living with anxiety and fear, which ultimately helped me to face the biggest unknown of my life.

Finding out that I had stage IV cancer, when initially I was told I had an infected gland and then told I had a small, benign tumor was shocking. The word cancer, and whatever thoughts I had about it based on my own limited experience and perceptions, was quite disturbing to me. The fear of the unknown from that point on were the many unknowns of cancer as a whole and my particular cancer which was rare and was lacking in necessary information for the doctor's to know how to best help me.

The unknown's grew by the moment; how treatment would affect me or help me and how fast the cancer would over take my body and result in my death is what I had to face. After my second surgery I was told that all the cancer was not removed and there was no way to know when it would progress to unmanageable. The prognosis was unsettling and disheartening. The fear of the unknown felt like a dagger pierced within my gut that fed up through my heart. It was as if every time I moved, breathed or woke up from a sound sleep the weight of this pain was there, like a heavy weight crushing me.

Dealing with my diagnosis and prognosis, living in emotional and physical pain was not easy nor is there a simple five step process to deal with facing the fear of this type of unknown. I was devastated, depressed and hopeless to the point of feeling suicidal. Yet, during the process of facing my fear, I realized that my past, my story, had prepared me for this very situation! I began to put thoughts and experiences of my past together to understand how and what I could do to handle this crisis.

I spent time doing research for ways to heal. I cried, I screamed and I wrote my thoughts down when I felt as if no one in the world had been through what I was facing or that anyone would understand. At one point I began to sense an inner strength that I never knew I had, but one that had brought me through so much turmoil since being a child. I learned through sharing my story from childhood to being diagnosed with cancer that others were inspired and encouraged by what I had endured and overcome. The best gift of all was the knowledge that my story mattered, that

I mattered. I realized that regardless of when my last breathe was breathed, my life had been purposeful.

I encourage you, through discovering your strengths and weaknesses, to find the ways that you can best face your fears of the unknown. My wish for you is that you can recognize, from your own story, that you too have overcome things and you have an inner strength of your own to face any fear before you.

—Angela Schaefers,
Writer, Speaker, Radio Show Producer and Host
www.yourstorymatters.net

I hope Angela's story inspires you to believe you too have that same champion within you and that you step boldly onto the pathway of inner enlightenment to personal freedom. Your story does matter and what matters even more is that you have the power to pick up your love pen and create a fearless masterpiece called your life.

I know one of the main reasons you are reading this book is to discover how to conquer your fears to live more fearless. You have bravely brought your fears to the surface thus determining where you are in this moment. The next step is to determine where you want to end up and how you are going to arrive at your destination. As you begin creating the vision for your fearless life, remember that there is no true destination and that your whole life is an endless journey. So be mindful to create stepping stones and guideposts to measure the success of your journey instead of a concrete point of arrival.

Creating Your Fearless Life Vision

If you could eliminate all of your fears and live the life of your dreams what would it look and feel like? I believe this question will require you to be braver than bringing your fears to the surface. It takes a lot of clarity, confidence and courage to envision the life you dream of and of course fearless action to bring it to life. Identifying your fears is essential; envisioning your fearless life and doing the work from the inside out to manifest it is critical because your life depends on it.

This is your moment to be very intentional and specific and get crystal clear about you want BE, SHOW UP and LIVE your life. Be bold, fearless and get creative. Let your imagination and heart do the speaking as you create your vision.

Reflection Questions to Create Your Vision

Find a peaceful place, be still and imagine yourself living the courageous life you desire and dream of as you reflect upon the following questions:

- How would you feel?
- What kind of thoughts would you have?
- Who would be a part of your life?
- Who wouldn't be a part of your life?
- What kind of work would you do?
- How would you celebrate you and your life?
- How much money would you make?
- What kind of house would you live in?
- What kind of car would you drive?
- How would you spend your free time?
- How would you take care of yourself?
- How would you live out your purpose?
- How would you revive your spirit?
- How would you experience more laughter and bliss?
- What kind of legacy would you create?
- How would spend your money?
- What kind of social events would you be involved in?
- How would you create peace and joy?
- How would you creatively express your passions?
- What type of training or education would you get?
- How would you invest in your business or professional development?

- Where would you travel to?
- Where would you live?
- What does the inside of your home look like?
- How would you give back to the world?

Fearless Action Moment

Take a few minutes and write a paragraph or two describing the fearless vision for your life based upon your responses to these questions. Use the space below and this prompt may help you begin your writing.

The vision for my fearless life is...

How does it feel to have the power to choose the responses to these questions? If you are feeling like it's a lot of work and a bit overwhelming I challenge you to look at it from a new perspective. If you see this opportunity as "too much mental" work then you may not be ready to live fearlessly. You see, the truth is, the real you is buried underneath layers of old, non-productive thoughts and habits. I want you to see this exercise as an opportunity to create new, productive and rewarding habits. I want you to see all of the exercises in this book as a splendid opportunity to go on a personal adventure of re-discovering you and awakening the Geni(us) within.

While doing more than just reading this book is highly encouraged, I realize you may be experiencing some internal resistance to change, some whispers of doubt or skepticism. If this is your experience it's perfectly normal and actually expected when you begin to create change. If you are ready to take the next leap that's wonderful. So whether you're feeling doubtful or eager and excited to move on, I want to offer you some affirmations to say to yourself as you continue on this journey. These simple yet effective affirmations will remind you of your personal power and help you begin to break down those old, negative thinking patterns that have served you no good.

Affirmations for Your Journey

I am powerful.

I trust my ability to create what I desire.

I always make decisions that serve my highest purpose.

I know what I need.

I can do anything if I choose.

I love myself.

I can change my life with positive thoughts.

I am courageous and I deserve to live my dreams.

You can do this, I believe in you. Trust that you are powerful, creative, wise, intuitive, loving, deserving and courageous! If at any time you feel stuck and or are questioning your courage come back to these affirmations and say them silently or out loud. They will help you find the strength, faith and courage to stay on the journey.

Now that you have answered those essential fearless life questions there's a set of other questions to consider. I know how easy it is to put a dream on paper yet never take the steps to making it a reality. Before I fully embraced my fearless personal power, I too wrote goals and dreams down but was still afraid to take the steps. So take a few moments and review the paragraphs you wrote describing your fearless life vision and ponder these questions.

What specifically is keeping you from living this fearless life now?

What kind of thoughts?

What behaviors?

Which people?

Which beliefs?

What obligations?

What past events?

What can you do right now to shift your thoughts, feelings and behaviors to begin creating this life right now, where you are with what you have?

As you transition into the next phase of mastering *The Art of Fear-Free Living*, know that you've just done some fantastic mental, emotional and spiritual work. You are already brave simply by reading this book and making it this far in the journey. Remember anything you do to improve the quality of your life is not work yet is an act of self-love. Right now you are honoring your value and making a personal investment in your life that will provide you with a life time of rewards. It may not seem like it now but again trust you, trust your ability, trust your strength and trust the process. It's taken a life time of experiences, thoughts and behavior to get to where you are right now and so living fearless will take some time too.

The unknown is waiting for you and I encourage you to begin seeing the unknown as an opportunity to again start and continue on a personal adventure of re-discovering you to awaken the Geni(us) within. In the next chapter you'll be challenged to make one of the biggest promises ever with BIG rewards... Are you ready?

"Nothing in life is to be feared,
it is only to be understood."

—*Marie Curie*

FOUR
THE MAGICAL PROMISE

*T*HERE ARE MANY PROMISES YOU WILL MAKE DURING YOUR LIFETIME. YOU'LL PROMISE GOD THAT YOU WILL SERVE HIM AND THIS IS THE MOST IMPORTANT PROMISE YOU CAN MAKE AND DEDICATE YOUR ENERGY TO. YOU MAY PROMISE YOUR PARTNER OR SPOUSE THAT YOU WILL ALWAYS LOVE THEM UNTIL DEATH DO YOU PART. YOU MAY PROMISE YOUR CHILDREN THAT YOU WILL ALWAYS LOVE AND BE THERE FOR THEM NO MATTER WHAT. I SUSPECT THAT YOU'VE MADE PROMISES TO FRIENDS AS WELL ABOUT WHAT YOU WILL DO FOR THEM OR HOW YOU WILL ALWAYS SUPPORT THEM. PROMISES, PROMISES WE ALL MAKE THEM AND IF WE ARE COMMITTED WE KEEP THEM. I BET YOU'VE MADE PROMISES TO YOURSELF THAT YOU WOULD READ MORE, LOVE DEEPER, LOSE WEIGHT, GO BACK TO SCHOOL AND A SLEW OF OTHER HEART ASPIRATIONS RIGHT? I KNOW EXACTLY WHAT THAT FEELS LIKE AND I ADMIT THERE ARE MANY THAT I DID NOT KEEP.

There is one promise I made to myself three years ago, a magical one. One that gave me the courage and inspiration to hop on my magic carpet and take the adventure of a life time and I am still enjoying the ride. I made a promise that

I would completely and fully let go of the past and all that it included. This didn't mean that I totally forgot about everything that happened to me yet it meant that I know longer allowed the past events of my life to determine the quantity and quality of my life to be determined by it. I promised that would not blame those who hurt me because I allowed the hurt to occur. I promised that I would not relive the past because it was stealing my joy. I promised that I wouldn't hold grudges against those who hurt me, deceived me, lied to me and or took me for granted. I realized while I was holding on and keeping my life captive they had moved on and were enjoying life as if we never met. I promised myself that I would allow healing to pour over my wounds because I deserved to be free of misery, worry and pain. I promised myself that I would put myself first, forgive myself and love myself unconditionally with absolutely no strings attached. I made this magical promise to myself because I got sick and tired of being sick and tired and I knew I deserved better and more.

Over the past three years I've done what I call "pulling weeds and planting seeds." I uprooted all the weeds (people, places, events, obligations, feelings, thoughts etc.) that keep me from seeing the beauty in my garden, my life. Pulling weeds and planting seeds allowed me to be very clear on what's important and focus on that which I desire to give energy to. When you choose to make the magical promise to yourself you will find yourself in a similar situation that requires you to make difficult but necessary choices. You'll begin to mindfully choose who you trust and share space with. You'll choose who gets the honor of sitting the front row of your life show. You'll choose how you spend your time and learn how to teach other people to respect it.

A Feather in My Hat

When I decided to leave my full time job and live my passion and purpose I had friends and family who thought I had lost my mind. They thought I was crazy and selfish because I was the bread-winner and I did not have 6 months worth of income saved like the experts suggest. They were confused and wondered what the hell had gotten into me. Some said "are you serious" while others just looked at me confused and startled like a deer in headlights. I was afraid as heck but knew deep in my gut like Carla, Amy and Angela that I had to do it and do it afraid.

When I started being very selective and protective of my time and energy, some of them got a little "pissy," and I could feel the vibes of "who does she think she is" vibrating in my direction. I feared losing some folks, and others, it was simply their time to go. Some folks had a hard time adjusting to this new found command of respect for my time. People would call me and ask for a ride, they would ask me to run errands and or want me to spend all my time talking on the phone about nothing really simply because I worked in my pajamas and didn't have anything important to do like go to a job. I learned very quickly how to say no, mean it and not apologize for it. It didn't take long for those folks to stop calling or at least make their requests in advance as a way of showing respect for my time. Saying no and getting the respect I deserved was a feather in my hat; today I proudly and courageously fan them out like a beautiful peacock! *I made a promise to put myself first, to fill my cup and serve others from my overflow...*

Making this one promise to myself has been such a liberating, empowering and satisfying experience. It took some time and definitely a lot of courage but it was worth the ups and downs. You can make that same promise to yourself right now in this moment or you can hurry through this book, pick out the golden nuggets and find yourself right back in this chapter wishing you had. Are you ready to make the biggest most magical promise ever? Are you willing to potentially lose to gain your life? Are you courageous enough to finally and truly put YOU first? This promise comes with risk and reward. You may be able to reduce the sting of your risk by making each risk calculated but then again there are some choices that you'll have no control over the outcome.

Let's try to put this choice into perspective so you can see what you are potentially about to experience. Take a few minutes and write down what you have to lose by taking the risks below:

If you take the risk what will you lose?

Saying no_____

Honoring my time _____

Protecting my energy _____

Leaving my job _____

Commanding respect _____

Saying yes when I want to _____

Focusing on what matters to me _____

Doing what my soul is calling me to do _____

Putting myself first _____

Now let's look at the other potential outcome with the same risks. Take a few minutes and write down what you have to lose by NOT taking the risks below:

If you take the risk what will you lose?

Saying no _____

Honoring my time _____

Protecting my energy _____

Leaving my job _____

Commanding respect _____

Saying yes when I want to _____

Focusing on what matters to me _____

Doing what my soul is calling me to do _____

Putting myself first _____

I'm not a psychic but the Genie within me says it's probably pretty clear what you have to lose and what you will gain depending on the choice you make. The magic question is which outcome will you choose?

When you start living for you, putting yourself first, saying no and meaning it and commanding that people respect your time and energy you won't be the most popular woman on the block, but what will happen is that you will finally step into being authentic. You will discover, embrace and own your personal power and set yourself free from the expectations of those around you.

Authenticity a word that's tossed around like a garden salad yet many people do not really understand what the word means and more importantly how to live authentically. I offer you a partial list of characteristics and traits of one who is living an authentic life. See how many of these describe you.

Authentic people...

- Know who they are in their core without hesitation.
- Are comfortable in their own skin.
- Accept their limitations and celebrate their strengths.
- Speak, act and live in integrity.
- Say what they mean and mean what they say.
- Show up in the world without masks, facades or costumes.
- Show you that what you see is what you get.
- Speak their truth even when it may hurt and do it with compassion.

- Engage with people without ulterior motives.
- Know and live by their core values.
- Treat people the way they want to be treated.
- Are the same every time you engage with them.
- Don't worry about what other people think of them.
- Do what they love and love what they do.
- Make it a priority to put themselves first.
- Don't change how they act in different situations.
- Live life on their own terms.
- Do what they say they are going to do.
- Are not afraid to simply be themselves.

Living authentically is a choice and always has been. It just may have not been a choice that you put great value on. I don't know about you but when I just look at that list I feel free so you can imagine what it feels like to live that list. An essential step in mastering *The Art of Fear-Free Living* is learning to live an authentic life with no apologies, shame, guilt or regrets. Easier said than done, I know but it is possible. Linda's story is one of many; a story of a woman who chose to authenticate her life.

COMING FULL CIRCLE

Linda Joy's Story

The past twenty-plus years have taken me on an amazing journey of self-discovery. I've moved through a rainbow variety of life experiences, some of which have filled me with intense joy and gratitude, and others which have sucked me into the deepest depths of self-doubt, pain, and despair. Like many on the path of self-actualization, I have fallen—and yet, somehow, each time I have found that core of inner strength which helped me to struggle to my feet, brush myself off, and move on. In hindsight, I can see that what I previously perceived as my biggest screw-ups have in fact been my truest and best lessons.

Some days, when I look back at my life, I giggle at the humor of the Universe.

On the first leg of my journey, during which I went from high school dropout and runaway to single twenty-two year old welfare mom—oh, and let's not forget financial misfit—I subconsciously labeled myself a failure. My mom dubbed me "the Queen of Self-Sabotage." When friends and family would ask me when I was going to do something with my life, I was prepared with a long list of reasons (which I now see were just excuses) why I didn't and couldn't and wouldn't have a chance at a life like that. I had spent so long viewing my life through a lens of shame and self-degradation that by the time I turned twenty-six I had already labeled myself a failure, and turned my back on the dream of a better life.

In the introduction of my anthology, A Juicy, Joyful Life, I share the emotional and intimate moment I experienced on a spring day in 1991. That moment became the catalyst for me to take back my life and launch my quest to reclaim my authentic self. From that day forth, I spent every spare moment reading inspirational books from leading spiritual visionaries like Norman Vincent Peale, Florence Scovel Shinn, Napoleon Hill, and more. These authors became my virtual mentors. As the years unfolded, I added to my transformational toolkit, soaking up the wisdom of teachers like Marianne Williamson, Debbie Ford, and Cheryl Richardson, to name a few. I dedicated myself to healing the cracked lens through which I viewed my life, so that I could create a better future for myself and my six-year old daughter.

The written word became both my solace and my impetus for change. The wisdom contained within the books I chose seemed to come to me just when I needed it most. Whether it was a word, a sentence, or a paragraph, each message that leaped off the pages at me was exactly what I needed to hear at that time, and gave me the fuel to move forward. Each day I thank authors and speakers like my virtual mentors who step through their fears to bring their wisdom, insights, and gifts to the world; they are beacons, shining their lights for others, like myself, to follow through their own darkness.

In many media interviews, I've been asked how I have continuously stepped through my fears and out of my comfort zone to transform my personal, professional, and spiritual life. I can't offer any direct advice; I can only share my truth and what's worked for me. To move forward, I had to accept that change and transformation in our lives have the power to grip us in paralyzing fear—but only if we focus on the fear. When I shifted my focus away from the fear, I discovered that no matter how difficult the road ahead might look, the thought of not living authentically and following my soul's purpose was far more frightening than the thought of moving forward.

After many years of internal work, I am able to view my past through a new lens—a lens shaped from hope, love, and the belief that anything is possible. Today, I look at my life and realize that every one of the extraordinary obstacles and perceived failures was really a stepping stone on the path to my authentic self. But it wasn't until I changed my perspective—my lens—that was able to fully experience the inner transformation necessary to create the outer change I desired. Changing the lens doesn't mean that I no longer experience ups and downs, disappointments or setbacks. But it did mean that when those things happen, I am able to rely on my passion and authenticity to give me the strength to get up and try again. The world was never against me, and it never will be. The only one who could ever defeat me was myself.

Today, I pinch myself often, just to be sure I'm not dreaming. In my role as Founder and Publisher of Aspire Magazine and President of Inspired Living Publishing, I am able to bring the words, wisdom, and insights of today's leading visionaries to women all around the world, with the intent to inspire them to live deeper, more authentic, and more grace-filled lives. Over the last five years, some of my greatest mentors have graced the cover of Aspire, including Marianne Williamson, Debbie Ford, Cheryl Richardson, and Dr. Judith Orloff.

Talk about coming full circle!

(And the Universe giggles...)

—Linda Joy
www.linda-joy.com

In many media interviews, I've been asked how I have continuously stepped through my fears and out of my comfort zone to transform my personal, professional, and spiritual life. I can't offer any direct advice; I can only share my truth and what's worked for me. To move forward, I had to accept that change

THE ART OF FEAR-FREE LIVING

and transformation in our lives have the power to grip us in paralyzing fear—but only if we focus on the fear. When I shifted my focus away from the fear, I discovered that no matter how difficult the road ahead might look, the thought of not living authentically and following my soul's purpose was far more frightening than the thought of moving forward.

A new lens, isn't that a refreshing perspective? What if you had the power to experience a new perspective on your life and how it can be? What if it was as easy as popping in a new pair of rose-colored contact lenses that allowed you to see and feel the magnificence of your personal power? With these new lenses you could create magic at your command, you could leap over challenges with confidence and courage or you could simply "be" in your skin being who you are, doing what you love and living life on your own terms. You don't need those contact lenses if you make the magical promise to yourself.

Today is a new canvas, a blank page in the story of your life. What will you choose? Will you continue to go through life trying to be everything to everybody, will you continue to adorn yourself with the masks of *"false-pride, fake it until you make it and I'm fine my life is okay"* or will you go to your secret hiding place and dig out all of those facades and throw them out with the trash? I am certain those masks shield the secrets of your soul and they allow you to show up in the world without revealing the true essence of who you are including the pain and struggle. I am certain those masks allow you to forget just for a moment that you have some unresolved issues, ghosts of the past and lingering limiting beliefs that keep your Genie under lock and key. Oh yes, I am certain of this because I had my stash of masks too. I know exactly how easy it is to slap a mask on, show up in the world and wiggle and squirm in my own skin. I also know what it feels like to then return home and unveil myself to reveal the real me. Yes, forced again to deal with and accept the reality of what's really going on in my life. I know how ridiculous, exhausting and pitiful it is to repeat this over and over again, beat myself up mentally for it and promise that I'd never do it again. These moments didn't happen often but when they did it was painful nevertheless. I didn't have this façade problem with friends and family but I sure knew how to play the game at work and in the world.

Slowly but surely I begin to pay attention to the drain and strain this created in my life and decided to listen to the all knowing voice inside that said "I created you perfectly unique just be you." I began testing this voice in reality by showing up a little more authentic each day and to my surprise most people embraced it while others were momentarily paralyzed by the assertion of my true self. Over time some people got use to it and others were forced to look at themselves and examine their authenticity. While I don't know their exact thoughts, I do know that if they accepted the real me they were welcome to stay in my life and if they didn't, with no regrets I let them leave. As the old saying goes "misery loves company" and that was not the company I wanted to keep any more.

So as friends, acquaintances, co-workers, partners and family members have come and gone, I still remain true to who I am and ever evolving into my most authentic self. Sure it was painful to watch some of them go but there is truth to the notion that people come into your life for a reason, a season or a life time. Regardless of the duration they are there to teach us something about ourselves. As painful and disheartening as some of the relationships are there is still a lesson. We become empowered when we learn the lesson, apply it to our lives and keep it moving. We become defeated when we linger in the past, blame ourselves, wallowing in the what-ifs and holding on to a relationship that has physically expired.

This is the moment! One that requires you to exercise great insight, acceptance and courage. Being authentic can be a challenge but as Ellie Drake says, "it's easier done than said." The biggest challenge for you will be whether you have the courage to examine who you are from the inside out and decide if you like who you are? When you are all one and in your most natural state are you satisfied? When you take off the suit and wash off the makeup do you still feel important and beautiful? When you strip away titles such as mom, wife, sister, daughter, friend or co-worker do you still have value? If you answered yes to all three of these questions then move forward with living the magical promise. If you said no to any of the questions you've got some more work to do.

It's possible to reach the place where you are ready to make the promise. Here are the key elements to the promise. Review them and see if you are ready to seal the deal.

- You are ready to completely and fully let go of the past and all that it includes.
- You are ready to no longer blame those who hurt you.

- You commit to not relive the past because it's stealing your joy.
- You commit to not hold grudges against those who hurt, deceived, lied to you or took you for granted.
- You are ready to allow healing to pour over your wounds because you deserve to be free of misery, worry and pain.
- You promise to put yourself first, forgive yourself and love yourself unconditionally.

Don't become overwhelmed by the list. Decide which one you can work on right now and put your full energy and intention into it until you master it and it becomes a natural way of being for you. Then choose another one and repeat the process until you can do them all with ease and grace. The beauty in the process is that by mastering each one you will have begun to live authentically. One of my favorite quotes by Ralph Waldo Emerson says "What lies behind us and what lies before us are tiny matters compared to what lies within us." Trust me when I say everything you need to master *The Art of Fear-Free Living* and be authentic lies within you. Trust yourself and believe it. If you have a tough time trusting yourself, trust your source because you were created powerful beyond measure. You came into this world with a Geni(us) so activate her and let her work her magic.

Remember, I said that living authentically comes with risk and reward. The risks are that you may lose some "friends" in the process, you may have to leave an unhealthy relationship, you may have to walk away from a job that does not feed your soul, you may have to step into the unknown and many other possibilities exist in taking risks. The rewards will be you'll know who your true friends are, you'll attract people who are like-minded, you'll be free of the pain that unhealthy relationships bring, you'll be doing work you love and you'll learn how to fly when you thought it was impossible. The list of rewards is too long to list but as you can see in the stories of these brave, ordinary women they found the light in the midst of darkness. They prevailed when they thought fear would steal their life. They lived to share the possibility and the power of choosing to show up as your authentic self and follow the guidance of your Genie.

Your magical promise doesn't have to be like mine or like the women in this book. It can't be because your life is yours and unique to you. You don't have to take the steps exactly as suggested but you do need to take steps with intention, belief, consistency and persistence. Your outcome will not be like any woman on the planet. Your experience will have its own flavor and so be mindful to not judge your success or compare your journey to anyone else's. This is the very reason why mastering *The Art of Fear-Free Living* is an art. You are the artist and with the tools to co-create already within you all you need to do is release your Geni(us), exercise your courage and paint the vision for your life.

> *"Free yourself from the expectations of others on how you should BE, LIVE, WORK or RUN your business. Do it your way, on your own terms and as long as you are co-creating with God that's all that matters."*
>
> —Catrice M. Jackson

FIVE
IT'S YOUR LIFE...
OWN IT AND CREATE IT!

*T*HIS IS YOUR MOMENT TO BE BRAVE, COURAGEOUS, BOLD AND FEARLESS. IT'S TIME TO DO THE WORK TO CREATE THAT BEAUTIFUL VISION YOU'VE CREATED. YOU CAN OFTEN TELL WHAT A PERSON REALLY BELIEVES ABOUT THEMSELVES ON THE INSIDE BY THE WAY THEY SHOW UP IN THE WORLD AND HOW THEY BEHAVE WITH SELF AND OTHERS. IN MY 6-WEEK AUDIO/VIDEO COURSE THE *ART OF FEAR-FREE LIVING*, IN STEP TWO I HELP PARTICIPANTS MIND THEIR MINDSET.

As you begin to create your fearless vision and execute your fear-free living plan you too will need to learn how to mind your mindset. In this chapter, you will learn how to get out of your heart and emotions and get into your head to create the change you want to experience, honestly face and deal with your stinking thinking and identify roadblocks, mental clutter, limiting beliefs and false evidence to disprove your irrational fears.

IT'S YOUR LIFE, OWN IT!

"Personal power is the ability to take action."

—*Anthony Robbins*

One of the greatest lessons I've learned is that my life is the result of my thoughts, feelings and actions. The first time I heard this I thought to myself "no, that's not completely true." However, after I really examined my life and the choices I've made it was clear to me that the statement was in fact true. It was hard for me to swallow at first because it meant that I had to take responsibility for the mistakes, the pain, the worry and the misery that once filled my life. Accepting this statement as truth meant that I had to hold myself accountable not only for my past, but my current life and the life I desired to live.

Only you can determine the direction, content and quality of your life. The very first thing you need to do if you want to create the life of your dreams, your best life is stop blaming other people for the quality of your life and take your life into your hands and own it. It belongs to you, it's yours and you can either own it or continue to let other people live your life for you.

When I speak about your life, I'm talking about every aspect of your life; your career, your finances, your relationships and your spirituality. When you take ownership of your career you begin to do work you love instead of working a job. When you take ownership of your finances you realize abundance is already yours instead of worrying about money. When you take ownership of your relationships you shift your focus from how other people are ruining your life and place it on how you are allowing them to ruin your life. When you take ownership of your spirituality you realize that a power greater than yourself is not outside of you yet within you always guiding you in the right direction. To own something is to accept it, embrace it, take control of it, be responsible for it and care for it. That's exactly what I want you to commit to right now. I want you to accept yourself just as you are. I want you to embrace your strengths and limitations. I want you to take back your life from all the things and people that are sucking the life out of you. I want you be responsible for how you think, feel and behave. Most importantly, I want you to really begin to care for yourself as you care for others.

You are absolutely the expert on your life, you are the Geni(us) so stop looking outside of yourself for the answers; they are within you. Now don't get me wrong there will be and are many people who can enhance your life but at the end of the day it's you who thinks your thoughts, feels your feelings and acts out your needs, wants and desires. You've heard the old adage that "you can lead a horse to water but you can't make it drink," well that is true about being the Geni(us) in your life. You can hire a coach, talk to your spiritual leaders and get advice from your family but when push comes to shove it's you who will drink or not. So are your ready to drink or continue to be led?

Let me lead you down another path to consider before you take your BIG sip of the sweet life. I realize that it is difficult for people to really understand what it means to "own" their life. I've also discovered through coaching many women that it's easier for them to identify what they don't want out of life and or how they do not want to show up in the world. There are some pretty standard signs that indicate whether someone is owning or disowning their life. Take a look at these five classic signs and see how much ownership you are taking for your life.

Five Signs That You Are Not Owning Your Life

1. You are stuck in the past and failing to create your now and tomorrow.

2. You are blaming other people for the current status of your life.

3. You are letting other people determine how your life should be lived.

4. You are waiting for the approval of others to make decisions and choices in your life.

5. You are contemplating everything about your life. You are stuck in place and not moving forward towards your dreams.

Even if you are experiencing only one of these indicators, you do not fully own your life. When you own your life that past has no credence in who you are and what you deserve. When you own your life you take full responsibility for your life. When you own your life you are in the driver's seat of your life and driving the darn car. When you own your life you don't wait for approval you create your life on your own terms. When you own your life you are moving freely, faithfully and fearlessly towards your dreams. If you are experiencing more than one of these indicators you are on your way to owning your life simply by reading this book. You must do more than read this book you must apply the strategies provided in this book into your daily living. Owning your life can be scary, frustrating and maybe even daunting. My response to those feelings and thoughts are this... own it or keep living it like it is. It's that simple. So if you are ready to completely own your life keep reading. If you are afraid to take responsibility for creating a life you love keep reading anyway, I am sure you'll find the inspiration and courage to awaken your Geni(us).

Five Things You Can Do Right Now to Begin Owning Your Life

1. Begin to forgive yourself. Forgive yourself for the mistakes you've made, the people you've hurt, the lies you've told and all the other things that brought you pain or pain to others.

2. Forfeit in the game of blame. Get up from the game, walk away and never play the game again. If you do you are guaranteed to lose. It's your life own it!

3. Make the magical promise to yourself and stick to it. You deserve it, your family and relationships deserve it. Everybody wins when you create the magic. Refuse to make excuses. Excuses are the doorway to failure and lack of fulfillment.

4. Decide what you want and fearlessly go after it. Move from thinking about your dream and start living your dream right now. You can be successful right where you are and who you are in this moment. Don't wait for everything to be perfect, take steps in the dark and follow your soul's voice.

5. Get yourself out of the way. Do not allow your inner critic to talk you out of your goals, dreams and aspirations. Get in the driver's seat and choose where you are going, how you will get there, who is going on the journey and who is staying behind and fill the trunk with everything you need to create success because failure in a fearlessly delicious life is not an option.

You may be thinking, yeah right, how am I supposed to do all that? You do it the same way you eat an elephant, one bite at a time. Be gentle with yourself and take baby steps if you need to. Some action is better than no action at all. My hope is that by the time you finish reading this book and applying the strategies to your life you will be more equipped to be and do all of these things; only if you choose. The most effective thing you can do to begin owning your life is to begin owning and re-creating you're your thoughts. Remember fear resides in your mind and it is there where you have the most power. Here's an example of how I learned to "own" my life by owning my thoughts.

Owning and Re-creating Your Thoughts

When I first started out on my business journey as a solopreneur I was eager to connect with as many women as possible. I just knew I had a great message to share with the world and that any woman would love to hear it. I soon realized a few things. I found out pretty quickly that my message did not resonate with everyone and for some my (what I thought was excitement) approach to sharing it was too aggressive. There were even moments when women did not want to connect with me; for what reasons I was not always sure. I began to get frustrated and disappointed and allowed my "stinking thinking" to set in. I had thoughts like "what am I doing wrong, they must be jealous, why wouldn't people want to hear about my passion, forget them I don't need them anyway." Sound familiar? Yes, I let my thoughts, negative thinking and even my ego propel me into this crazy concoction of poor me and forget the world. I can laugh at that now but believe me when I say I was being wildly tossed around in this tornado of stinking thinking. Before I knew it, I was angry, frustrated, mad, sad and confused.

There I sat on my pity pot wallowing in what I thought at the time was personal defeat. I questioned my motives, replayed my thoughts and repeated this several times over a period of days. What I realized later on was that I allowed my thoughts to throw me in the dark pit of fear. I was afraid I was being misunderstood, I was afraid I was ruining my reputation, I was afraid people would not like me and I was afraid that I would not create the success I desired. While preparing for a psychology class I was teaching, I ran across a handout on thinking errors and sat quietly reading them and realized what I had done to myself with the power of thought. I made it a point to begin learning more about the power of thought and how to re-structure my thinking to achieve the outcomes I desired. I also made it a point to learn more about social networking and how to show up in the virtual world in a different, more authentic way. So I share with you what I've learned based my own experiences, studying and research. Now, when stinking thinking (thinking errors) shows up I know exactly what to do even when I am afraid.

These thinking errors or "stinking thinking" can keep you in a vicious cycle of self-defeat and fear. We all have them and some of us allow them to control our lives while others know when they show up and are able to mind their mindset to prevent the stinking thinking from taking over.

Stinking Thinking Thoughts
that Keep Your Geni(us) in the Bottle

☐ You make a big deal out of trivial things.

☐ You have the tendency exaggerate your thoughts and blow them out of proportion.

☐ Your thoughts tend to come from one end of the thought continuum or the other (right or wrong, good or bad and or black or white).

☐ You fail to see the middle ground or grey area in your thoughts or the thoughts of others.

☐ You worry about things happening before they do and with little evidence that they will.

☐ You generalize everything and your favorite words are never and always.

☐ You have a hard time seeing and accepting other people's perspectives.

☐ You think you know what people are thinking and make assumptions about people.

☐ You're constantly thinking the worst things will happen.

☐ You fail to see small successes and focus on the negative.

☐ You think the world revolves around you and fail to see and appreciate the experiences of others.

☐ You often think about who is bigger, better, smarter and richer.

☐ You think that your job, lack of finances, and/or friends or family are the reasons you are frustrated, unhappy or miserable.

☐ You believe people don't appreciate you and if they would your life would be better.

☐ You think that your self-sacrificing behaviors will eventually pay off when people realize your value.

☐ You blame the world or yourself for the circumstances in your life.

☐ You often use statements that use I should, I could, I must, I need, I ought to and or why didn't I.

☐ You desire to be right and have no problem telling others when they are wrong.

I don't claim to know everything but I know that anyone who consistently thinks like the examples above is sure to also think negatively about themselves and their life. Negative thoughts breed negative emotions and negative emotions fuel negative behaviors. The way you think directly effects your emotions and feelings. If you are consistently feeling sad, you are thinking sad thoughts. If you often feel angry you are thinking angry thoughts. On the other hand if you feel happy you have been thinking happy thoughts. Have you noticed when you are in your groove, feeling good and loving life and then all of a sudden you get a phone call that's disturbing or you receive a past due bill in the mail, how your mood quickly sinks into sadness, sulking and suffering? This has happened to me many times and still does on occasion. I can tell you what goes through my mind at the time. I begin to think somehow I need to sympathize with caller on the disturbing call or I allow their experience to get in my head and the next thing you know I have hopped on the negative bandwagon. When that past due bill would arrive I'd go into a panic frenzy and worry about whether I had the money to pay the bill or not. A slew of thoughts would run through my mind and just like that I gave my mental power away. Sound familiar?

What I learned to do was to choose to not engage in the negative conversation or emotionally and mentally activate my SHero Shield and only absorb what I wanted and deflect the rest. This allowed me to be available for my friend or family member but not let their situation siphon out my emotional energy. Each time I did this I felt powerful, in charge and more confident to do it the next time. I also learned how to not let money and bills determine the quality of my life but it took some time.

FROM MONEY-FOCUSED TO MISSION-DRIVEN

Before I left my full-time job I was making pretty good money, didn't worry about bills, had health and dental insurance and was living with little financial stress and struggle. I had read many times that before leaving your job to start a business you should save at least 6 months of income to have as start up and living funds. I originally started my business in 2005 after being laid off from work twice in a row. I knew then I had to put my financial security in my own hands. I started putting together my business plan and had a decent foundation set for my speaking, training and consulting company. There was something comforting about knowing I could be in control of my life, time, freedom and finances. However, it was more comforting at the time to rely on a steady flow of income so after the second lay off I looked for a job and found one that paid me well.

I was now working at the full-time job that I eventually left before starting my business. I went in early, stayed late, volunteered to be on committees, took on extra projects, developed programs, served on the management team and wrote grants to bring large amounts of money into the organization. I put my heart, soul, blood, sweat and tears into developing a diversity program that not only pulled in a hefty amount of grant dollars but brought amazing, positive attention to the program. The program was going well until I suggested that we as an organization do what we asked other organizations to do; work on strengthening our commitment to a particular cause so we could walk the walk.

It started off spectacular but turned sour very quickly when the personal expectations and challenges became too great for the staff. It was clear to me that many of them only wanted to talk about it but didn't want to be about it. I went from SHero in the blink of an eye. Deep in my soul I always knew there was something greater I was supposed to do in life. I knew with every fiber of my being that I had a gift that was sitting on the back shelf because I was afraid to step out of my financial comfort zone. I was convinced that employer after employer had no clue of the value I brought to their organization. I knew that I was a pawn in a chess game set up for me to never really win. I was tired of working my butt off to raise someone else's revenue. I was tired of creating winning programs to only leave all my intellectual property behind. I was sick and tired of being sick and tired.

In the winter of 2007 I went in for a routine doctor's visit. I am anemic and had not been taking my iron pills. I knew my doctor was going to take blood samples and she would get on me about not following her orders. After the appointment, I stopped by the local pharmacy, picked up some iron pills and went back home. Once I got home I checked my messages and the first one I received was from my doctor. The message went a little something like this "Catrice, your hemoglobin is extremely low I need you to come back in and check into the hospital." I went into a state of panic and worry and immediately went back to the hospital. I was informed my hemoglobin was 5.5 and the normal range for women was between 12 and 16. Basically I was "walking dead." Hemoglobin carries oxygen to your organs and major organs such as your brain and heart.

I was presented with two options; go home and work on getting my hemoglobin up by myself or take a blood transfusion. I couldn't take the risk of failing to raise my hemoglobin so I decided to get the blood transfusion. It was not an easy choice. My late grandmother always preached about how it was a sin to take

76

body parts and fluids from another human being and that God didn't like that. I found myself in a spiritual dilemma and finally made the decision to go through with the transfusion. I made the choice because I wanted to live, I wanted to be around for my son and husband, and I wanted to live out my dreams.

While lying there watching the first drop of someone else's blood go into my veins, I prayed and begged God to let this procedure be complication free. All the life changing questions went through my mind, "am I living on purpose, am I doing God's will for my life, am I living out my purpose and dreams etc." The answers to all of those questions was no. I prayed to God to give me another chance to live and to do what my soul was calling me to do. God answered my prayers abundantly. I experienced a "Soul Eruption" (the spawning of my first book entitled *Soul Eruption*, released in 2009).

I woke up from the procedure, went home and said "this is it, it's now or never." I spent most of Saturday talking to God, praising him, thanking him and asking for faith and courage. I spent most of the day Sunday drafting my resignation letter and experienced a great amount of relief, pleasure and "knowing." On Monday, I went into my boss's office and said "I've decided to resign to live my dreams." I gave her a two month notice and planned my dream work and worked my plan. The last two months of employment were daunting. I wanted to leave and they wanted me to leave. They didn't want me challenging their beliefs and actions and bringing to the surface how they were not fulfilling the mission of the organization. It was evident how much I was valued and appreciated and I vowed to never give my gifts away to anyone who did not appreciate them. I learned valuable lessons in my employment history but I learned the most rewarding lessons in the three months prior starting my business. The greatest nugget of all was that it was more important to do work I love regardless of how much money I made. I thank God for enlightening me to move from a money-focused way of living to a mission-driven way of being.

This *Soul Eruption*, the chaos and craziness of this situation taught me a few things; 1.) Money is not everything, 2.) Doing work you love is much more rewarding and fulfilling, and 3.) To put less focus on money and more emphasis on serving and sharing my gifts with the world. I've learned when you live on purpose your provisions will be met. I trust God more than ever to manage my bank account. I realize that I am the money and I have the ability and gifts to create prosperity. I know for sure that answering and fulfilling my soul calling is more important than a six-figure income. I have arrived at this place because I mindfully mind my mindset, I don't allow my inner critic to have a front row seat in my life story and I know how to turn my stinking thinking into power thoughts that produce the desires of my heart.

I regret nothing. All of the experiences leading up to writing this book has shaped me into the woman that I am and strive to become. My history has helped rise into resilience, leap into loving me as I am and courageously create the life I am living. When you own your mind and create your thoughts you create your life, create your destiny and create your legacy. My story is not unique, many women just like you chose to do work they love knowing that when they genuinely serve the world from their heart the money will come. Shann Vander Leek is a witness to this powerful moment of enlightenment.

LETTING GO OF THE CONVENTIONAL CORPORATE WORLD

Shann Vander Leek's Story

Not long ago, my career had been dedicated to selling, training, mentoring and leading an exceptional television advertising sales force.

For most of my prior professional career, 1 was a woman who: was happily married, earned a six figure income, was a loyal employee, was an over achiever, traveled to exotic places, would live in my dream home, and wanted to be involved in the highly charged corporate world forever!

Things change...

A sacred knowing or astuteness accompanies the first foray into motherhood. Children have a way of smacking you upside the head with an uber dose of what is truly critical. Having a daughter became the catalyst for a complete lifestyle transformation. The high stress of being corporate Shann and doing business in someone else's boardroom was losing its appeal. Even though the chosen path resulted in the realization of my goals and dreams, I quickly became completely disinterested in corporate culture and, unwilling to jump through any more hoops for a fat paycheck. I simply had to let go of the only career I'd ever known.

It's amusing, and disheartening, when you realize your dedication, smart work, energy,—all the things you put into your career daily—are ONLY for the sake of performing a duty and receiving a paycheck. This awareness helped cement my corporate world exit strategy. It was time to let go of the illusion of control that the "big bucks" created.

I started preparing my exit strategy. No longer a company creature; my job was surely destroying my soul. I longed to spend my days being left alone by the "powers that be". After much thoughtful consideration, conversation with my husband and confidantes, moving forward on the path of my dreams as an entrepreneur was the only choice.

For about one year, many of my evenings, weekends and lunch hours were dedicated to self improvement and earning my professional coaching certification. This due diligence included, setting a new household budget, moving investments, setting up a home equity line of credit, and finally, buying a new car (for the first time in 11 years!) The plan was to build my coaching business and the *True Balance Life Coaching* brand, one day at a time until I could give my two weeks' notice.

After fourteen years , I let go of the corporate life on my terms. My former employer decided to downsize our management group within two months of my planned exodus. The choice of who would leave was ours to figure out amongst ourselves. I volunteered to be the "lucky" laid off executive and have never looked back. Thankfully, this scenario meant an unexpected severance and benefits package from my former employer. Synchronicity is such a blessing!

I packed my box, said so long to the big bucks, turned in my company SUV, let go of a cushy expense account, and found the courage to walk away from a career that no longer suited me.

Fast-forward ...

Today I am a woman who is grateful to have a healthy and happy daughter, who has earned the six figure income plus all the perks, who has traveled to many delightful places, who currently lives in the home of my dreams, and who has become a successful entrepreneur, transition coach and published author.

Letting go of my ties to the corporate world allowed me to create a coaching business dedicated to supporting powerful women in transition, who wish to accelerate life on their terms and create more balance in their lives. All the characteristics that made me a success in the conventional business arena benefit me as an entrepreneur and life on your terms accelerator. I am eternally grateful to follow my passion while supporting others to do the same.

What I love about Shann's story is she courageously faced the unknown by trusting her Geni(us) and rested faithfully in the knowing that all was well even in the eye of the storm. No matter who you are or where you are in your life you too can trust your Geni(us) and allow her to be your guide towards creating and living a life you absolutely love; one that nourishes and fills your soul and serves the world at the same time.

—*Shann Vander Leek*
International Transition Coach
www.shannvanderleek.com

It's your turn again. It's time for you to mind your mindset, re-create your thoughts and step into the knowing of your life. Here's another opportunity to get in touch with your Geni(us) your SHero. Yes you must listen to your gut, yes you must follow your heart but you also must quiet that inner critic, stop the stinking thinking and breakdown those mental roadblocks that are creating mind clutter, fostering limiting belief and keeping you on the fear freeway.

Take some time to work through the following exercises. Each one is designed to help you gain more clarity on exactly how to awaken your Geni(us) and create your fearless life.

What kind of stinking thinking are you willing to admit to?

How is this stinking thinking creating fear and stress in your life?

Are the source of the thoughts real or imagined? (Do you have tangible proof that the thoughts are true about you?)

What are the top 5 emotions or feelings you experience in a typical week?

In an average week how many times do you experience the following feelings/emotions?

- ☐ Fear
- ☐ Anger
- ☐ Sadness
- ☐ Jealousy
- ☐ Envy
- ☐ Apathy
- ☐ Worry
- ☐ Anxiety
- ☐ Doubt
- ☐ Exhaustion

- ☐ Satisfaction
- ☐ Joy
- ☐ Happiness
- ☐ Peace
- ☐ Excitement
- ☐ Passion
- ☐ Fulfillment
- ☐ Hope
- ☐ Faith

Specifically list the source(s) of the negative feelings/emotions you experience.

Specifically list the source(s) of the positive feelings/emotions you experience.

How are these thoughts and feelings keeping you stuck in fear?

How would you like to think and feel in a typical week?

What can you do right now to re-create your thoughts and feelings to experience what you really desire in life?

Congratulations to you for taking another huge leap towards learning how to master The *Art of Fear-Free Living*. Your Geni(us) is rising to the top of the bottle and is one step closer to emerging from captivity. Fearless living is possible when you view your life as an adventure, tell the truth about who you, what you desire and courageous acts of fearlessness in every moment of your life. Take time everyday to discover, re-discover and embrace what you are passionate about. Let go of all things that drain you and move you away from your purpose. A fearlessly delicious life is waiting for you to boldly step into it with ease and grace and you can do it when you silence your ShEgo and release your SHero.

Discovering your passion and creating a luscious life is really about letting go and allowing for grace through the transition.

—*Shann Vander Leek*

SIX

SILENCE YOUR SHEGO AND GIVE VOICE TO YOUR SHERO

*W*ITHIN EACH OF US LIVES A SHEGO AND A SHERO. WE WERE BORN WITH ONE AND LIFE CREATED THE OTHER. THE SHERO IS THE HERO WITHIN US. IT IS OUR WISE EYE, OUR INTUITIVE VOICE OUR COURAGE COMPASS, OUR CHAMPION. SHEROES DO NOT MAKE EXCUSES THEY TAKE FULL RESPONSIBILITY FOR THEIR LIVES. THE SHEGO ON THE OTHER HAND, OPERATES FROM A VICTIM STANCE AND FINDS EVERY EXCUSE POSSIBLE FOR NOT CREATING THE LIFE SHE DESIRES.

Making excuses is the first cousin of stinking thinking and can be just as paralyzing. Excuses are the doorway to failure and key to an unsatisfied life. If it's your intention to fail and live an unfulfilled life just keep making excuses and you'll get just that. I've made many excuses in my life and from time to time find myself on the excuse excursion even today. Excuses keep us safe but unsatisfied. Excuses keep us comfortable but never courageous. Excuses, excuses, excuses aren't you tired of making excuses? I am and therefore am very mindful to realize when I begin to make them and have learned that excuses are the fumes of fear. I've learned to closely examine the excuses and go directly to the fear from which they result.

In this chapter you'll receive insightful and practical strategies from Step Three of the Mastering *The Art of Fear-Free Living* life empowerment course. You'll learn how to silence your ShEgo and give voice to your SHero. Your ShEgo is full of excuses and allows her ego to reign in her queendom. I can say pretty confidently that if you don't move your ego out of the way you will remain in a fearful state and stay stuck in your life. This is the moment in the journey where you embrace your excuses and eliminate them. My hope for you is that you discover how you are in your own way even when you think you are not and commit to becoming excuse-free to empower your life. Excuses are the fumes of fear so where there are excuses there is fear flaming under the surface. As the old saying goes "where there is smoke there is fire."

Excuses or reasons NOT to do something are the doorway to failure. A successful person knows they must do certain things they do not want to do or know how to do in order to achieve success. I believe you want to successfully create and live a fearless life. In order to do that you MUST eliminate the excuses to open the door to your fear-free life.

Here are a few truths about excuses:

- They are harmful and keep you from succeeding.

- If used often enough they become a limiting belief.

- Once they become a limiting belief they become anchored in your heart/spirit (feelings) and show up (your behaviors) in your life as obstacles and or unfulfilling ways of being.

- You fail to take responsibility for your failure or success.

- You live a mediocre life instead of extraordinary life.

- You blame other people for the quality of your life.

- You sit on the side lines of your life instead of being the superstar on your court of life.

A courageous and fearless life is not created with an excuse-filled mindset. I do understand that you may have been hurt, disappointed, taken for granted and or even abused in some way; yet out of your pain there is possibility, in your misery there are miracles and in your mess there is a message. Creating and living a fearless life is a choice. Will your choice be to let your circumstances captivate you or will your choice be to allow your circumstances to be your launching pad to a life with passion, purpose and prosperity? There is a magic carpet circling the Universe waiting on your command to land and take you on the adventure of a life time; the adventure of discovering, embracing and releasing your Geni(us). Before you hop on for the ride of your life it's time to eliminate the excuses.

Now it's time to pull out all of your excuses! Excuses come in many disguises and may not always show up as an obvious excuse. I want you to think about two or three things you really want to do and then think about why you are not doing them. Take a few moments and write down three things (goals, dreams or aspirations) you really want to do in the near future.

3 Goals, Dreams or Aspirations

1.
2.
3.

Now use the space below to list the excuses or reasons for why you are not doing them or taking steps towards making them happen. Be honest or fear will reign!

Reasons/Excuses for Not Taking Action

How are these excuses/reasons serving or *de*-serving you?

What is the real "fear" underneath the excuses?

What can you do to take responsibility and turn the excuse into an action?

Here are some practical actions to stop making excuses and take responsibility for your success!

1. Living fearless is a choice. Either take responsibility for your life or let your fears and other people determine the quality of your life.

2. Simply put, stop making excuses! They are boldly leading you down the path of failure, fear and dissatisfaction.

3. When you find yourself making an excuse ask yourself this question "what am I afraid of?" Identify the fear and embrace it. Then use everything that you've learned about conquering your fears to move through the fear.

4. Imagine how much better your life will be if you make the choice to do what you are avoiding doing.

5. Talk yourself into doing the things you need to do instead of talking yourself out of them.

6. Remember to use the "what is the worst thing that could happen" technique if you DO or DO NOT take action as a way to inspire ACTION. Often times you will have made it worse in your head than it really is.

7. Look back on your life and see how "making excuses" has kept you a prisoner within your own skin. You do not want to repeat this behavior.

8. When you find yourself making an excuse ask yourself this question "Am I afraid of success?" If you are, discover why and work through that.

9. Just do it and do it afraid if you have to.

When you eliminate the excuses (reasons to fail or not take action) in your life it can propel you forward in ways you can't imagine. Although Aimee was afraid to face her excuses, she pushed through them, eliminated them and fully expressed who she was.

"He who is not everyday conquering some fear has not learned the secret of life."

—Ralph Waldo Emerson

FEAR OF FULL SELF EXPRESSION

Aimee Yawnick's Story

I had just taken my coaching practice from hobby status to real entrepreneurial status, and hired a mentor with whom I really resonated with her business model. I was thrilled to have a plan! There was only one problem; the business model included public speaking. My fear of being seen in public was paralyzing. I never liked to be the center of attention. What if I blew it? Worse yet, what if I actually succeeded? Then what?

I began to realize that there were a lot of factors at play here. I was being called to do something I encourage my clients to do every day. Stretch beyond your comfort zone. What kind of mentor would I be if I let fear stop me from doing the same? I was also at a place in my business where I knew if I didn't make this happen, there was a good chance my business would not survive and I would eventually have to close my doors. That was not an option.

I was at my emotional pain threshold. In an instant I knew that the pain of not fulfilling my purpose was far worse than the made up pain in my head about what would happen if I spoke in public. The fear was not real. So I made a choice. I chose to trust that I am divinely guided to share my purpose in this new way. And by stepping out of my comfort zone, I was saying. "Yes!" to my brilliance and light and to playing a bigger game.

I haven't looked back since. The experience of speaking in front of that first group was so inspiring and fulfilling. To serve more than one woman at a time was invigorating! If you know that speaking to groups is the next step in your journey remember this: Your DREAMS are STRONGER than any false fears. Your audience needs what you have to share in only the way that YOU can share it.

If I can do this, YOU can do this.

—Aimee Yawnick,
Needham, MA
http://www.coregrowthanddevelopment.com/

I appreciate Aimee's story because she did not allow excuses to keep her from facing her fear of speaking. She also was fearless enough to walk the walk instead of talking the talk. It took a lot of honesty and courage for her to do what she expected her clients to do. Aimee made magic happen in her life by choosing to pick up her magic wand and wave it bravely in the direction of success. Identifying and eliminating your excuses is only a piece of the magical puzzle. There's another life stealer you need to be aware of that may be keeping you captivated in fear; your ego.

An understanding of what the ego is and how it functions in your life is essential to awakening your Geni(us) because "she" at her best does not operate and show up in the world from an egotistical stance. Sigmund Freud, a renowned psychiatrist from Vienna, introduced the world to the ego, id and superego. Freud believed that the ego was one component of our personality that served as the regulator or the middleman to our id and superego. The ego serves two psychological purposes: 1.) to keep us from acting out our impulses or innate animalistic urges and 2.) To create a sense of harmony or balance between our personal values and morals and the morals and expectations of society. The ego is at work in our subconscious and conscious minds and can be our keeper, as well as the culprit to our demise.

Freud further speaks about our "ego defense mechanisms" and how they serve to protect us and sometimes keep us in denial of reality. He coined several specific defense mechanisms and to learn more about them I suggest you do some research on the works of Sigmund Freud. My goal in sharing this information with you is simply to give you a psychological backdrop to why we as humans do the things we do. Now at first glance the ego appears to serve you well and it does, however the ego can also get in the way you experiencing life the way you truly desire. The ego does this best by utilizing "ego defense mechanisms" as a way to keep you stuck or keep you safe. We'll examine how safe and stuck may also be keeping you in fear.

In my work with adolescents in drug addiction treatment is where I was able to see these defense mechanisms in full effect. Those with additions are masters of defense because defending their drug use or abuse keeps them from dealing with the reality of change and sobriety. This is also true for anyone avoiding dealing with the realities of their lives and or those needing to make changes in their life. So this theory and these defense mechanisms apply to all of us regardless if we have an addiction or not.

When anxiety arises in your life and you are faced with a dilemma of change the easiest thing to do sometimes is to deny that a problem even exists. Denial is one of the most common defense mechanisms used and keeps you safe because you don't have to face the potential danger or pain of your unsatisfying life. Denial also keeps you stuck because if you deny that there is a problem, you don't address the problem and the problem either continues to exist or grows. In this case, the defense mechanism of denial serves you no good.

Another defense mechanism that shows up often is rationalization. This is very similar to making excuses or giving reasons as to why you should not change or how change is not going to work for you. When you find reasons for not taking action in your life and you give reason as to why you cannot make the changes you are rationalizing your life. Again this defense mechanism keeps you executing excuses instead of executing your personal power.

Suppression is another unproductive defense mechanism. Suppression occurs when you bite your tongue, hold back your thoughts and choose to not speak your truth. Suppression if not managed well can lead to depression. If you continually hold in your thoughts, feelings, ideas or comments they have nowhere to go and result in a dark, heavy, lonely place thus creating depression. It's unhealthy to live in suppression. A fearless life is one that encourages you to find your authentic voice, your truth and speak it. When you speak your authentic voice you honor your value and show the world that you have value and what you have to say has value too. When you suppress your authentic voice you ultimately say to the universe I do not deserve to be heard, your opinion doesn't matter and you are to be seen and not heard. Living in suppression is a very dis-empowering place to be and if you are living in this space the only motive of suppression is to avoid the anxiety and or potential backlash of speaking up; a perfect example of living in fear.

These defense mechanisms do serve an important role in your psychological health, however overuse of them keeps you from facing your reality and dealing with your fears. As you can see by the examples above too much denial, rationalization, and suppression can cause you to "zone out" and or live on auto-pilot. If you live this way your Geni(us) will remain dormant and bottled up. The good news is now that you are aware they exist, you have been empowered. You now have to move beyond being empowered and take inspired action to break down the walls of defense that detour your destiny. You are the main character in your life story and living your life "in defense" keeps you behind the curtain and even backstage. It's time for you to take another brave step and honestly identify how your ego defense mechanisms are sabotaging your success. It's time for YOU to get out of your own way...

Real Life Examples of How Your Ego is in the Way

- You know you need help, support and or a coach/ mentor but are afraid to ask for fear of being perceived as weak.
  - You stay stuck.
- You see someone making great strides in their life and experiencing success yet you choose not to congratulate them.
  - You miss the opportunity to learn from them and grow.

- You focus on how much money you make and choose to not see the other value and contribution you bring to the world.
  - You miss out on the beauty and brilliance of just "being."
- You view those who do not have a formal education or higher education as being lazy and ignorant.
  - You miss the opportunity to see the human spirit.
- You don't let people into your circle because they don't have the credentials, expertise, financial prosperity or material belongings you have.
  - You miss the opportunity to receive the special gifts they possess.
- You make excuses for people you love and care about and attempt to be their rescuer.
  - You stagnate their growth and stroke your ego in an unhealthy way that does a disservice to them and you.

How are your "ego defenses" in the way of your success?

How do denial, rationalization and suppression show up in your life and keep your Geni(us) captive?

Defense mechanisms are another example of fumes. Remember where there is smoke there is fire (fear).

How can you begin to break down the walls of defense and take responsibility for your life?

If you desire your SHero to reign in your queendom you must silence your ShEgo and become the master of your mind. As the slogan for the United Negro College Fund says "*A mind is a terrible thing to waste.*" When you allow your mind to be wasted on worry, doubt, and fear you waste your life and find yourself living with regret. Don't take your goals and hopes to your grave, don't let your dreams die within you. You are a special gift to the world and it is ready, willing and waiting to unwrap your brilliance. Get up, get out of your way, get into the game of your life (instead of sitting on the sidelines) and get busy creating and living your victorious life!

"Your mindset will make you miss your miracles or make them happen. Quit sitting on the sideline of your life and get in the game! You're on the sideline, if you are waiting, contemplating, procrastinating and waiting for 'it' to fall out of the sky and land in your lap. Stop making excuses and create your fearless life."

—*Catriceology*

SEVEN

TRUST YOUR SHERO
SHE IS ALWAYS RIGHT

I BELIEVE THAT IT IS SOMETIMES EASIER FOR PEOPLE TO TRUST OTHERS THAN IT IS TO TRUST THEMSELVES. ISN'T THAT AMAZING YET RIDICULOUS? WELL IT'S TRUE AND I KNOW BECAUSE I HAVE EXPERIENCED PUTTING MORE FAITH AND TRUST IN OTHERS YET STRUGGLED TO TRUST MYSELF. AWAKENING YOUR GENI(US) IS ANCHORED IN TRUSTING YOURSELF. IF YOU CANNOT FIND THE COURAGE TO HAVE FAITH IN YOU AND TRUST THAT YOU KNOW WHAT YOU NEED YOU WON'T BE ABLE TO MASTER THE *ART OF FEAR-FREE LIVING*.

In 2007, I had the wonderful opportunity to participate in a women's leadership conference. One of the table exercises was to discover our core values. They handed out a sheet of paper with a list of several words such as joy, peace, laughter, service, and family to name a few. We were instructed to choose 15 words that described what was important in our lives. We were then told to choose only 10 from the 15 we chose and eventually we had to decide which of the 15 words would be our top 3 values. It was slightly difficult but when I listened to what mattered most in my heart and spirit instead of choosing what I thought would be "right answers" I made an authentic decision. These words were not simply words but they were values we chose to use as the guiding principles for our lives. The three words I chose were integrity, peace and inspiration. From that day forward I vowed that I would live by my core values in every moment.

While I knew I had core values before, these 3 words took on a whole new and profound meaning in my life. I have always been a woman of high integrity and so it was no surprise that integrity was my number one choice. Growing up in a family with many faces of chaos, I despised it with a passion and knew that I would create a peaceful home for my children and my life. I guess I wasn't too shocked that peace was my second choice. I was a little stumped by inspiration. I wasn't quite sure I knew how to fit that one into the context of my life but after I thought about it I have always sought out inspiration and was perceived as inspirational to many people at a very young age. Many times people would tell me how they admired my courage and outspoken spirit. I just thought I was being myself and didn't really see anything special about it.

I realized I had the gift of inspiration when I did my first public speaking engagement. It was like I was watching myself on a movie screen as I really looked into the eyes of the audience and saw they were engaged and hanging on every word I said. It was in that moment that I knew God had given me the gift of voice and spoken word. After reflecting on this inspiration is a must have in my life. I need to be inspired, I desire to inspire and inspiration is embedded in the fabric of my being. I now use these core values to navigate my way through life. I use them to choose friends, business partners and make decisions about what I choose to give my time and energy to. If a person, event, and or opportunity does not feed those core values, I choose to not engage.

I used to say yes to many things and many people but now I intentionally focus on and give energy to things that really matter and honor my core values. This awakening of my power to choose has liberated my spirit, de-cluttered my mind and allowed me to preserve and protect my emotional energy. Much of the work in mastering *The Art of Fear-Free Living* is mental work but there is a tremendous amount of emotional and spiritual work involved as well.

While I realize the bulk of this inside job (living fear-free) is mental work it is important to do the necessary work within your heart and soul (or spirit). When you choose to live fear-free it has to anchor in what your heart and soul desires. "In your soul lies your dreams, desires and the source for divine living. Fearlessly release your juicy goodness (secret success ingredient) and bring forth your BIG dreams and your secret desires. Living in fear will suffocate them. Values are beliefs that determine what you feel, think, need, want and desire out of your life. These values dictate how you spend your time in this moment and they are anchored in "what matters most to you."

Let's begin by identifying your core values—what matters most in terms of how you live your life. Core values can be described as guideposts or standards for how you want to BE and LIVE. Take a few minutes and review the Core Value List and choose 15 values that resonate most with you. Then choose 10 from the 15 and finally make your choices for your top 3 core values.

Core Value List

Love	Family	Adventure
Joy	Peace	Integrity
Inner Peace	Intimacy	Intelligence
Honesty	Passion	Motivation
Achievement	Comfort	Beauty
Creativity	Courage	Travel
Success	Spirituality	Respect
Leadership	Learning	Faith
Independence	Belonging	Purpose
Happiness	Relaxation	Confidence
Abundance	Fame	Serenity
Grace	Healing	Recognition
Faith	Wisdom	Excitement
Exploration	Inspiration	Empowerment
Nature	Diversity	Simplicity
Harmony	Freedom	Health
Play	Reliability	Patience
Curiosity	Charity	Service
Friendship	Excellence	Prosperity

If you do not see one that matters to you include it in the list

What Are Your 3 Core Values?

1.

2.

3.

Why are they important and why did you choose them?

How will you begin to use them be in your Geni(us)?

Now that you have determined what your core values are in this moment let's talk about how to use them as a catalyst for creating your fearless life. First let me say that more often than not your values will primarily stay the same over time. However, if they change it only means that you are successfully re-inventing yourself and thus your true core values will evolve into the 3 you refuse to live without. Once they show up, embrace them and use them as your compass for living.

My dear friend and colleague, Lorna Blake did this same exercise in essence in her own life as she was faced with the choice to either stay comfortable or break free in her life. Her decision to listen to her heart and follow its lead was a courageous one. Here's her story of choosing to live by her core values.

WHEN THE HEART SPEAKS LISTEN

Lorna Blake's Story

It was the end of 1992 and I was working at an insurance company as an accounting clerk. It was a good job with excellent benefits and I was a single mom with a one year old baby. I had just returned to work after maternity leave and I took time to reflect on how I felt about the work I was doing. I learned that as much as I enjoyed the support of a wonderful group of colleagues, liked working with numbers and loved the benefits provided by my company, my work wasn't stimulating and challenging enough.

I realized that I wanted to work with people, helping them solve their problems. In that moment, I made the decision to quit the full-time job with great benefits and return to school full-time to get a Social Work degree. Many of my co-workers thought I was nuts or even downright irresponsible. Why would I leave a good job with benefits to go to the University full time just after starting a family? How was I going to live? What kind of quality of life could I offer my child if I wasn't working?

I was clear that my dreams were very important and that my pursuit of this particular dream would make me happy. I listened to their suggestions and advice but I made the decision anyway. These are some of the questions I asked myself to help me gain clarity. What are the things that I really want? What really makes me happy? How do I want to make a difference in the world?

I did research and asked God, the Universe to give me signs letting me know I was on the right track. One of the quotes that found its way to me was: *"When you come to the end of all the light you know and you're about to step off into the darkness of the unknown,* faith *is knowing that one of two things will happen. There will be something solid for you to stand on or you will be taught how to fly."*—Patrick Overton

I reaffirmed this every time worries or fears of uncertainty gripped me. I quit the job in September 1993 to pursue full-time studies at the University. I had never felt as inspired and motivated to go after my dreams as I did then. Did it make me happy? You bet! Was it easy? No, but it was exhilarating as hell. Would I do it again? Yes, I've done it several times since then.

I had to apply for student loans to pay for my education and it did become financially challenging. My baby was diagnosed with asthma when he was two years old and I spent many sleepless nights at hospital emergency rooms as he experienced frequent asthma attacks. I had to pull many all-nighters to meet my project deadlines. As if that wasn't enough I became pregnant at the end of my second year at school and I made the decision to have the baby and to stay in school.

Did I feel I was being guided all that time? I have no doubt that I was. Having taken this path back in 1993 made it easy for me to decide to leave another secure job and become an entrepreneur, Coach and Public Speaker some 15 years later. I always have the assurance that as I step off into the darkness of the unknown I'll be given wings to fly...

—*Lorna Blake,*
Life Coach, Speaker and Consultant
http://mpowerurself.com

I can certainly relate to Lorna's story because I was once in a similar situation. When the heart speaks you must listen and be courageous enough to follow its lead. I absolutely love the quote shared in Lorna's story and ironically, that same quote showed up in my life month's before I took the leap of faith. I didn't find the quote it found me as a sign of what was to come. I posted it on the front of my computer screen to remind me of the leap I would someday take. I looked at it every day and asked God to prepare me for the leap. I trusted he would and expected nothing less than soaring beautifully into my destiny. I said yes to my soul-calling, I said yes to my purpose, I said yes to my heart's desire and most importantly, I said yes to God's will for my life.

Maybe you are ready to say yes to all of those things. Maybe you are ready to courageously discover your soul's purpose. Knowing who you are and exactly why you were created is such an exhilarating and comforting experience. When you embrace this blessing it takes much of the struggle out of life, you know the path you are to walk and you spend less emotional energy trying to figure out the "what" in your life. Knowing your soul's purpose also requires you to know the "who" as well; who you are in your core your DNA. Both the who and the what rest patiently in your Geni(us) waiting for you to gently remove the Genie bottle top and let your SHero out. You are the co-creator of your life and when you fully focus on the who and the what, God takes care of the how and when; that's called living with ease and grace. I share with you a powerful exercise to discovering your soul's purpose so you can focus your time and energy on what really matters. Fill in the blanks with the answers that come from your heart.

Discovering Your Soul Purpose (What Matters Most)

I love _____

I am passionate about _____

I feel compassion toward _____

The greatest tragedy would be_____

I would really love to_____

I am enthused when _____

The most meaningful thing is _____

I am inspired by _____

I come alive when _____

I like to think about_____

I wonder why _____

If I could change one thing in the world
it would be_____

The most important thing in my life is _____

I value this most _____

My deepest wish is _____

I am most capable of _____

I have a special ability to _____

My greatest talent is _____

I would do this for free _____

I admire _____

I need this to feel complete _____

My dream job or career is _____

This gives me satisfaction _____

I need this to feel happy _____

This person would be a great mentor _____

I am willing to take a risk on _____

The vision for my life is _____

People say I am good at_____

People describe me as _____

I feel compelled to _____

It is right to _____

I feel connected to _____

I am creative when _____

My heart feels for _____

If you look closely at your responses you should see a theme that speaks to your heart and soul. These responses can be stepping stones towards discovering your "who and what" and hopefully even your passion and purpose. Another goal of this exercise is to help you to begin crafting your life mission and vision statement; the reason and purpose for your being and life. When your mission, vision and purpose is clear it increases your confidence to take steps forward in creating the life you desire.

In one statement, I want you to write a mission/vision/purpose statement for your life. An authentic statement should include your core values, the essence of what really matters to you and how you want to be, show up, and live your life. Be creative, have fun, write it from your heart and be brave enough to think big!

My Mission/Vision/Purpose Statement

_____

_____

_____

_____

_____

_____

_____

_____

_____

You've been learning how to face and conquer your fears, discovered your core values and created a vision statement for your life. My hope is that you are feeling much more hopeful, encouraged and inspired to fully embrace your SHero and be the Geni(us) you already are. It took a lot of courage to dig deep in your heart and put your vision on paper. Now that you see it in black and white how does it feel to see your dreams? If you didn't come up with a vision statement keep working at it and write what feels right in your spirit. If you did know that it may change as you continue to evolve as it should take on a new shape and feel as you grow. You are going to need a small group of trustworthy, unselfish and committed people to help you bring that dream to life; your dream team.

In chapter one, I talked about how when you begin to elevate to your highest self there will people who don't understand, become offended, walk out, feel left out and maybe even envy you. I wish I could tell you that this will not happen and I

THE ART OF FEAR-FREE LIVING

sure hope it doesn't yet just know it's highly likely. While it may not feel good while it's happening in the end your life will be more peaceful and fulfilling. Those kinds of situations are dripping with negative energy. The kind of energy that can steal your emotional energy; the fuel you'll need to create and live a fearless life. An essential skill you'll need to develop is learning how to preserve and restore your emotional energy. When your emotional energy tank is low or running on fumes you will not have the energy to focus on what really matters. This is where your dream team becomes priceless.

A dream team is one of the greatest blessings you can receive. This team of supporters should be there with you as you take steps to make your vision statement a life experience. They are a part of the experience and they dedicate a portion of their time to help you evolve into your highest self. The members must be chosen carefully and with full intention. I recommend that you begin taking notice of those people currently in your circle of influence and determine who has core values similar to yours. Pay attention to the people who are there when you need them with no expectations. Be mindful of the people who believe in you when you are unable to believe in yourself. Listen to the intuitive voice within you and pay attention to how you feel around certain people; especially those who make you smile, make you feel safe and those who allow you to be your authentic self. These types of people would make great dream team members. These are the people you'll want to give your emotional energy to.

If you don't have these kinds of people in your life, keep working on removing the energy stealers so you can make emotional and spiritual space for those who add value and meaning to your life. You'll also find it necessary to simply ask for and allow God to send you who you need and in many cases this is a better option. Start envisioning the kind of people you want in your life, be bold enough to ask for them to come, imagine them coming, believe they will and keep your spirit open by allowing them to show up when the time is right. In the meantime, be sure to preserve your emotional energy.

In my first two books, *Soul Eruption! An Amazing Journey of Self Discovery* and *Delicious! The Savvy Woman's Guide for Living a Sweet, Sassy and Satisfied Life,* I speak often about preserving your emotional energy. Here is an excerpt of what I mean and why it matters.

What is emotional energy really?

It is the invisible yet powerful source that governs our decisions, choices, actions and behaviors in life. Emotional energy is your life source. Without it we are zombies in life, living on auto pilot and missing out on the sweetness of life. Emotional energy is as essential as the air we breathe. When our emotional energy is depleted we emotionally die inside. Having significant emotional energy to sustain life is essential. Let me say it this way. You are the car. Your soul/spirit is your gas tank. Your emotional and spiritual energy is the gas. When your emotional energy is low you are cynical, doubtful, afraid, apprehensive and unhappy thus you cannot move forward.

The biggest energy stealers are fear, the inner critic, negative thinking, incongruency and toxic people in your life. The keys to preserving your emotional energy lie in these six bold and brave actions.

1. Conquer your fears and take control your life.

2. Silence your ShEgo and awaken your champion voice.

3. Choose to take fearless action in every moment.

4. Master your mindset, eliminate the stinking thinking and excuses to empower your life.

5. Discover your core values
    and live congruently authentic.

6. Pull weeds and plant seeds (remove the toxic people in your life and make room for people who will pour into your cup).

SHero Strategies to Preserve and Restore Your Emotional Energy

-   Always know that you have the power within to co-create your desired experiences.
-   Wake up that Geni(us) and let her work her magic.
-   When you feel afraid focus on what you can do instead of focusing on the fear.
-   Seek out resources to help you overcome your fears.
-   When you don't know what to do, do nothing, sit in silence and wait for your Geni(us) to order your next steps.

- Create reflection time and get back in touch with your soul purpose and listen to that intuitive voice.

- Only move or take steps towards that which elevates you to your highest self.

- Refuse to engage in negative situations and be intentional about who you spend time with.

- Do things you love and engage in activities that bring you joy.

- Share your thoughts and feelings with people you trust.

- Trust yourself you know what you need.

- Start eliminating obligations and give energy to the people and events that matter most.

- Be grateful for who you are and what you have. Keep a gratitude journal of all the good things and blessings in your life and reflect upon it often.

- Keep a list of all your successes and refer back to it when you think you can't win.

- Let go of the things you can't control and focus on what you can.

- Quit worrying about what you cannot control.

- Simplify and declutter your life to make room for all the amazing things ready to come into your life.

- Create "you time" every day and take care of your needs, wants and desires.

- Teach people how you want to be treated.

- Do not suppress your thoughts allow your Geni(us) to be released and appreciated.

- Live life in the now moment don't deny yourself the sweetness of life by living with regret.

Abraham Lincoln said *"In the end, it's not the years in your life that count; it's the life in your years that count."* If you don't start living the life you desire right now you will wake up one day and ask yourself "How did I get here in this place of stagnation, why am I here in a place of regret, why didn't I do something different, why didn't I live the life of my dreams."

Yesterday is long gone, tomorrow may never come and now is all you have. Refuse to allow excuses and fear to create your life and tell your ShEgo to set up camp somewhere else. Take brave steps in every moment. Hop on your magic carpet every day and go on the adventure of a lifetime; explore and discover who you are, why you are here, what you are called to do and how you can use your Geni(us) to serve the world. Trust your SHero she is always right.

"So, the path of the co-creator is to be awakened spiritually within, which then turns into your own deeper life purpose, which then makes you want to reach out and touch others in a way that expresses self and really evolves our communities and our world. Certainly, we can't do that unless we activate ourselves first. That's why, for me, emergence is the shift from ego to essence. That is so important."

—*Patrick Overton*

EIGHT
TAKE BACK YOUR POWER AND RECLAIM YOUR LIFE

*T*RUSTING YOUR SHERO EMPOWERS YOU TO RECLAIM AND STAND IN YOUR POWER. OUR PAST AND CURRENT STORIES OFTEN ILLUSTRATE OUR ABILITY TO TRUST OR NOT TRUST. EVERYONE HAS A STORY, EVERYONE HAS A ROLE IN THEIR STORY AND YOUR PERCEPTION OF YOUR LIFE IS YOUR REALITY. MAYBE THERE HAVE BEEN EVENTS IN YOUR PAST THAT EITHER WEAKENED OR STRENGTHENED YOUR ABILITY TO TRUST YOURSELF. MAYBE THERE HAVE BEEN EVENTS IN YOUR STORY WHERE YOUR TRUST WAS ABUSED, NOT VALUED AND UNDERAPPRECIATED. THOSE ARE REAL EXPERIENCES THAT HAVE BEEN PLANTED IN YOUR MIND, HEART AND SPIRIT. MAYBE THOSE EXPERIENCES HAVE BROKEN YOUR SPIRIT AND CAUSED YOU TO PUT UP A WALL OF PROTECTION.

I may not know your exact situation or know your pain but I know what it feels like to give deep from within your heart and to have someone mistreat your trust. I know what it feels like to love someone and not have them love you as much as you love them. I know how it feels to have someone take my love for granted and I know how it feels to have someone you love walk out of your life and not even tell you why or say goodbye. Story after story, pain after pain I too have been left in broken pieces wondering how I was going to go on in life. Story after story I blamed myself and questioned what I did wrong or what I could have done differently and mentally beat myself up over and over again. I spent moments crying, hiding in bed, praying, and even feeling numb and functioning on auto-pilot.

Over the years, I slowly began to forgive myself, forgive those who hurt me because deep inside I knew it wasn't my fault, somewhere deep inside I knew I had value and deserved better. Each time I was able to genuinely express forgiveness I liberated my life, my spirit became lighter, I experienced more peace and began to regain my power. Of course it sounds easier said than done and while I was wallowing in my very real pain I didn't think it was possible either.

There were two things that always kept me hopeful. Before the birth of my only son I talked and prayed to God. He never left me alone while I had forsaken him many times— when I needed him he was there. The one consistent message I received from God was *there is something greater in your life and this is simply preparation for your destiny.* I had no idea what that really meant and literally couldn't wrap my arms around this destiny he spoke of. Even though I knew I was created to do a special job I just couldn't make sense of it in mind or spirit. I decided to trust in something I couldn't see, feel or touch; that's called faith.

I continued to trust God and after the birth of my son I had something, someone else to believe in. Wow! What an amazing gift. Words cannot adequately express the feeling, the blessing and privilege of motherhood. If you are a mother

I'm sure you know exactly how I feel. God knew I needed something tangible to believe in, someone who would love me unconditionally and I the same. Motherhood blessed me with the opportunity to learn again how to love, trust and believe in something greater than myself. I thank God for this blessing everyday and I am grateful my son chose me to come through into this world. The gift of motherhood and my belief in God was the road to recovery; recovery from being a blame and shame addict. I chose to be thankful for everything I had. I chose to love again. I learned to trust in things I couldn't see. I learned to trust myself and each time I did I became stronger, wiser and more resilient. All my fears are not gone and occasionally they show up like a roaring tiger but I know God gave me the personal power, faith and courage to co-conquer anything and I trust in that knowing.

My friend Gayle has a story worth sharing. After reading her story I was in awe of her power, strength and will to not only survive but thrive. You have a story, I have a story; we all have a story. Our stories are unique yet the same. We live and love, we hurt and worry, we experience joy and pain, we lose ourselves in fear and in moments we are courageous. Never discount the reality of someone's story because we cannot feel what they feel or experience what they experience. I trust you know what your story feels like. I trust you know what you need and I trust you will be brave enough to allow yourself to have it. When you trust yourself and reclaim your power you reclaim your life. Gayle did it and so can you.

FEARFUL OF LIVING MY DREAM
BECAUSE OF FEAR ITSELF

Gayle Joplin Hall's Story

As a former victim of domestic violence, I was always fearful. In order to recognize fear and the association with abuse, one would have to understand a victim of domestic violence never knows when the next attack will occur—she just knows that it will. Anything can set her partner off and the battering begins all over again. Consequently, I lived in fear 24/7.

If you were to speak with me during a counseling, coaching, or consulting session, meet me on the street, or have ever been in my college classroom, you would more than likely say to yourself, "Wow, what an outspoken, witty, and intelligent woman." I am all of that, and more. My biggest secret, hidden from the world, is that I lived in fear, even though I have been out of the abusive relationship for more than 15 years. So now you must be asking yourself, "Why was this woman fearful if she was not being abused? Shouldn't the fear be absent?" The answer is, "No, the fear was not gone. I was still afraid... of everything."

During my recent doctorate, I interviewed therapists for my research who worked with victims and to my amazement, I learned something about myself. Typically throughout the inquiry, one will process data and arrive at an analysis about the study. Even though I came up with a conclusion for my research about the therapists, more significantly, I learned why I was so fearful about every single thing in my life.

Fear keeps a person on guard at all times. Fear and worry go hand-in-hand, so it is no wonder that I never had a good night's rest, suffered from Irritable Bowel Syndrome (IBS), Post-Traumatic

THE ART OF FEAR-FREE LIVING

Stress Disorder (PTSD), and Fibromyalgia for over 15 years. Just two years ago, I was diagnosed with Generalized Anxiety Disorder (GAD) and Obsessive Compulsive Disorder (OCD). One therapist made a comment about fear that really described my life. This was pivotal for me. Fear made me afraid and scared of everything in my life. Likewise, I came to the realization that anything I could not control, I was afraid of. I was never able to control my abuser as he lashed out at me. Therefore, I now needed to be in control of my life so I would not be afraid. Fear is controlling.

I was afraid of loving for fear of being left and cannot begin to tell you how many men I pushed away before they had a chance to even really know me. I was afraid of not being good enough, afraid of spending money or not having money, afraid of being attacked, afraid of getting lost, afraid of the dark, afraid of bugs, and afraid of being told again that I was worthless and stupid. I was mostly afraid of learning for fear of not being able to learn. For this reason, I stayed in jobs that I hated. I enjoy volunteer work. Helping others is my passion and when volunteering, nobody ever says, "You are not good enough." I did not have to be fearful. Nevertheless, something inside held me back from living my dream.

My dream was always to earn my PhD, become a professor, write books, and start my own counseling, coaching, and consulting business. Good parenting was my first priority when my children were young. I never went to college until I was 38. In business, I made good money, but was never satisfied because I was not living the life I had dreamed. As a professor, I loved this because I was helping students learn. Nonetheless, God was calling me to help people on a much larger scale.

Completing my research helped me realize why fear had driven my need for perfection in me for so long. Countless hours in research were completed far in advance of the due dates. This was normal for me because I had to be perfect. I typed two, 20-page research papers for two concurrent ten-week classes at the doctoral level, six weeks in advance, so as not to miss the due dates in case complications from a surgery ensued. As I look back now, I think, "How absurd!"

My three children are all grown now, however, in the past, I made unrealistic demands from them, as well as from friends, only to be disappointed. They have all come to realize I expected this perfection, not from them really, but from me at all times, without any flaws, or I would face the fear of disenchantment once again. I constantly lived in fear.

I have now learned that it is fine to be imperfect and that I will still be loved by those who truly love me. I am unafraid of venturing out in public without make-up and am not living in fear of what may happen if I do not cook a perfect meal or for that matter, choose to not cook at all. None of this could have taken place in my life one year ago because I had to be perfect. I lived in perpetual fear. I was scared and faced the fear of failure, fear of success, fear of yet another failed relationship, and fear of not being good enough.

My fears were so strong that they held me back from living my dream life. Why is fear so powerful? Fear interferes, but it does not interfere any longer. Today, I am still afraid of bugs and the dark, but I can proudly say that I am on my way to living a life free from fear!

So now you must be saying to yourself, "Please tell me how Gayle overcame fear to living her dream." Here are the four steps in the most simplistic format:

1. Acknowledge and recognize your fears.

If you do not understand what you are afraid of, you cannot work on overcoming your fear or fears. You must look your fear squarely in the face, name it, and then figure out the best way to get through it. For me, I had to hear a trigger word and that word was "control." When I recognized all of my fears were due to things I could not control, I comprehended for the first time in my life why I was the way I had been for over 15 years—a worrier and afraid of every single, little thing.

2. Know where to turn for help, or ask.

I am a Psychologist with a PhD, so I am smart, educated, and should be able to "fix" myself, right? No—this was wrong! I needed help from professionals and I needed it quickly. You see, I never hesitate once I make up my mind to do something. So once I realized I had a problem that caused all of my fears, worry, and anxiety, I understood I needed to see a specialist. I was embarrassed to seek help, so I asked a dear friend who is a nurse. Her staff would not accept my insurance. Another facility could not get me in for two months. I needed help and I needed it now. I knew that I needed help from the mental health arena.

I called my doctor who takes care of my fibromyalgia and he made a call for me to see the best Psychiatrist in the city. Before the visit, I received a 24-page document, asking for my medical history. When I met the Psychiatrist the following week, I was with him for three hours. I received the most thorough examination I have ever had. My parents did not agree with my treatment plan because I am now on prescription drugs and others may not think this is great either. You see, I take anti-anxiety medications and also take medication to help me with sleep and pain. For the first time in my life, I can say I am able to sleep at night without worrying all night long about the next day. I also use psychotherapy on myself. For me, this was and is the right choice. I also eat healthier foods and practice meditation. Each plan for help will vary and must be individualized. The important message to receive from this is to know you are not alone. Just ask for help.

3.   Stay on track to be successful at becoming fearless.

There are two sure-fire ways to stay on track. The first way is to set goals by having a good roadmap or blueprint. Set small, doable goals that are easy to maintain, and build up to long-term goals toward becoming fearless. Remember, you cannot see where you are going without a good roadmap. The second way is to surround yourself with like-minded people or others who will support you. Avoid anyone who will drag you down or keep you locked up with your fears.

4.   Believe you can live the life you have always dreamed of.

First and foremost, you must be able to see yourself living the life you have always dreamed of. This is so incredibly important. Use a piece of poster-board to create a "dream" board. Envision yourself living your beautiful life. Erase the fears by working through the previous steps and you will be on your way to fearless living and having the life you not only imagined, but have always dreamed of.

—Gayle Joplin Hall, PhD
Psychologist, Counselor, Life Coach, Consultant, Entrepreneur
www.HallWaystoHappiness.com and www.DrHallonCall.com.

126

Gayle certainly reclaimed her power and her life. I can confidently say Gayle realized her personal power was always within her and it is her life source. You have that same amazing source and it's the only thing you have control over. You exercise this power in every moment whether you realize it or not. You use it to create your thoughts, express or suppress your feelings, make decisions and choose how you are going show up in the world. The magic word is "choose." Everything that has happened, is happening and that which will happen will be the result of your choices to exercise or not exercise your personal power. There are moments when you own your power and there others when you give it away. Do you know when those moments are?

Signs You Are Giving Away Your Power

1. You worry often about how to make other people happy.

2. You have difficulty speaking your truth.

3. You hold your feelings in and express them only after you've had enough.

4. You blame other people for the quality of your life.

5. You say things to make people happy even when it's not the truth.

6. Your personality changes each time you are in a new setting.

7. You let other people's thoughts and choices dictate your life.

8. You are trying to live based on someone else's standards.

9. You are sitting on the fence of fear and not creating your life.

If you look closely at these signs you'll see that each one of them is attached to some kind of fear. The fears may range from fear of conflict, fear of being heard, fear of being authentic, fear of accountability and or fear of facing and living the truth.

How are you giving away your power?

How does it feel when you give your power away?

Signs You Are Embracing Your Power

1. You seek to please yourself first instead of others.

2. You say what you mean and mean what you say.

3. You speak from the heart and communicate directly.

4. When someone has offended you, tell them instead of holding it in.

5. You take responsibility for your life.

6. You are genuine with your words and actions.

7. You don't try to fit in, instead you show up as yourself.

8. You rarely make excuses and take action to create your dream life.

9. You are an independent thinker and honor your values.

If you look closely at these signs you'll see they are attached to some form of love. The expressions of love may include love of self, love of peace, love of your life and or love for others. There are a variety of ways love shows up in your thoughts and behaviors. Are you able to see how it shows up in your life?

How are you embracing your power?

How does it feel when you embrace your power?

The biggest power stealer is the elusive, cunning and wise inner critic. Listening to your inner critic is another form of giving your power away. The inner critic has many motives and one is to keep you powerless. Sometimes it can be so sneaky that your thoughts and voice become the voice of the inner critic. When *you* say things like "I can't because, I shouldn't because, I can't afford to, and or I wish I could," your inner critic adds things like "you're stupid, why did you let that happen, who is going to believe you, why should anyone hire you, you're too fat, why are you staying in this unhealthy relationship?"

So obviously the best way to take back your power and reclaim your life is to quiet or silence the inner critic. The most effective strategy for quieting or silencing the inner critic is to hear it and do the *opposite action*. Opposite action is when you do exactly what the inner critic says you can't do. So for example, if you have been wanting to write a book and your inner critic says things like "no one wants to hear your story or you don't have the skills to write a book" you would listen for a moment and immediately do the exact opposite. You would share your idea of writing a book with some trusted friends and see if they would be interested in reading your story. You would immediately sit down with paper and pen or at your computer and begin writing. This opposite action says to the inner critic "oh yes I can write a book and people do want to hear my story."

The sneaky inner critic may be silent for a while but it will creep back in and try to talk you out of finishing that book or attempt to distract you with other negative mental tapes and messages. However if you use this opposite action strategy immediately and consistently over time you will give the inner critic no choice but shut up or pack up and leave. Here's the truth about the inner critic. It will always be there. You can only decrease its intensity, frequency, duration and power. You can decrease the power by listening to it and not avoiding it. Facing it will take away the power. You can decrease the intensity by testing what it says you can't do by doing just that (reality testing). You can decrease the duration by hearing what it says, and immediately saying yes I can. In time the critic will only speak for a short time. You can also decrease the frequency by reducing its power, intensity and duration. Misery loves company and when you become happy and confident on the inside misery and doubt will move out.

Fear only speaks to you when there is something you really want and desire. Its main goal is to talk you out of getting it so it (fear) can have a place to live within you. When you use "opposite action" you take back your personal power. You must do the opposite action immediately or you still give away your power and before you know it, your inner critic will say "see I told you so." Keep adding actions immediately and repeatedly until the voice is eliminated. I guarantee that if you do this correctly the critic will stop speaking about how you can't do this or that. For the best results practice opposite action for each limiting belief or negative message that the inner critic whispers in your ear. Before you know it, you will have silenced that monkey mind in your head. You'll soon feel powerful again and equipped to allow your Geni(us) to help you tackle anything that comes your way and make your wishes come true.

If your inner Genie could grant you 3 wishes or dreams what would they be? What 3 things would you like to do, have or experience in the near future? Take a minute and think about those 3 things, the list how your inner critic is talking you out of having, doing or experiencing those things.

My 3 Genie Wishes

1.

2.

3.

How is my inner critic talking me out of these wishes?

Were you able to see how you might be giving your power away by entertaining and believing your inner critic? The only way you reclaim your power and take back your life is by courageously facing the inner critic and silencing its voice. I trust, know and believe that you know what you need and what you want in your life. I also believe that you deserve those three wishes and all of the other desires of your heart. Your Geni(us) is waiting to grant your wishes at every command. You can summon her any time you choose. You can take back your power any time you choose. You can rise out of the ashes of your circumstances wiser, braver and more fearless if you choose. You must be willing to silence the inner critic by listening to it, practicing opposite action and turning those negative messages into positive affirmation to fuel your dreams. I want you to trust yourself and allow your SHero to guide your steps towards bringing those wishes to life. What can you do right now to begin taking back your power? List your actions below.

_____
_____
_____
_____
_____
_____
_____
_____
_____
_____
_____

Remember... this is your life and your story. When the story of your life is written, lived and read by others will your pages be filled with fulfilled dreams or the saga of regret? Will the chapters bleed with sorrow, fear and complacency or will the joy, delight and satisfaction you experienced colorfully dance on the pages of your life? It's your choice, it's your life and your story. Embrace the power of your love pen and create a beautiful masterpiece and legacy.

"Listen to what you know instead of what you fear."

—*Richard Bach*

NINE

WHEN FEAR WALKS OUT LOVE RUSHES IN

*L*OVE IS THE MOST POWERFUL ENERGY SOURCE AVAILABLE TO WO(MAN) KIND. IT IS THE POSITIVE FORCE THAT IGNITES YOUR PASSIONS, PROPELS YOUR PURPOSE AND FUELS EVERYTHING THAT BRINGS YOU EXCITEMENT, PLEASURE AND JOY. LOVE IS NOT SOMETHING YOU SEEK OUT TO EXPERIENCE FOR LOVE IS WITHIN YOU. YOU ARE LOVE AND LOVE IS YOU AND THE SAME IS TRUE OF EVERY OTHER HUMAN BEING ON THE PLANET.

It's amazing how so many people, women in particular are on a relentless quest to find that someone who completes them, their soul mate. We think about love, dream about love, chase love and the pursuit of love becomes a daily ritual. Now, there is not anything so wrong about wanting to find someone to love you. We all want to be love, appreciated, and valued for who we are. We all want someone to accept us as we are and love us unconditionally.

I feel confident saying that outside of nutritional food, love is one thing people are hungry for on a daily basis. We crave attention, affection, compassion, acceptance, recognition and approval. We seek it from our family, friends, children, partners, co-workers, bosses, and society as a whole. While you may not admit that you are actively seeking it you are.

When you put your title behind your name this is a form of seeking recognition. When you ask others for their opinion you are seeking approval. When you snuggle up to the ones you love you are seeking affection. When you tell someone about your difficult day at work you are seeking compassion. There's nothing wrong with seeking these things because they are forms of love.

Take a minute and think about the last five sentences in the paragraph above. Do you realize how much mental, emotional, physical and spiritual energy you expend on a daily basis seeking love from outside sources? Yes, you too are hungry and on a relentless, often subconscious mission to find and receive love if you are brave enough. When you don't receive the affection, compassion, recognition and approval you've sought out, guess what happens? Typically, one will retreat, back off and immediately look within. The energy has now shifted from an outward hunger and quest to an inward starvation and moment of second guessing yourself. You may begin to wonder, what's wrong with me, what did I do wrong, don't I deserve all these things? If you fail to receive what you seek often enough you will stop seeking it all together and the starvation increases. In effort to feed your hunger, your spirit becomes desperate for any type of feel-good food to diminish the hunger pangs. You may turn to food, drugs, alcohol, pour yourself into your work, zone out or find yourself settling for any negative nugget of love you can get your hands on. If this pattern persists you may find yourself on an unplanned excursion of addiction, isolation, depression and or unhealthy relationships.

This detour does not have to be a part of your journey and if it already is there is an exit wide open, just ahead waiting for you to take the turn onto a better, healthier more fulfilling road. You're going to need some fuel for this new path, you're going to need the most powerful energy source in the world; love. The love I speak of is not the same approval, recognition and compassion you receive from other people. The fuel you need for mastering *The Art of Fear-Free Living* is a super juice called self-love.

If we back up to the previous example I shared about being rejected and not receiving the love you sought out, you'll see that self-love was not part of that equation. Someone with a healthy dose of self-love would have been hurt by the rejection but not hindered by it. A person with robust self-love would have known they deserved what they requested. They also would have loved themselves enough not to allow those destructive things to occur. They would have put more energy into loving themselves fully and first thus only allowing the right people to be in their lives. People who do love them unconditionally and willingly give recognition, approval, affection and compassion without being asked. If you find yourself or have been in this situation don't beat yourself up, it happens to many people, it happened to me. Remember, you always have the choice to start fresh with a new canvas every day.

Love is powerful, self-love is divine. The love you have for yourself is unconscious and conscious reflection of the love you expect to receive from others. Love regardless of its shape, form or flavor is a magnet that attracts unto you according the love you have for yourself. I learned that the hard way.

Remember my past story of young life without responsible, accountable men? Well, you guessed it, my mental tapes told me I was unlovable, unworthy and undeserving of men who would be around, take responsibility and be present in my life. I allowed my fear pen to write my early love stories which resulted in unhealthy relationships with men who were absent physically and emotionally and or who refused to be responsible and accountable. My low self-love covered up by false pride created the same old story in a different chapter. Finally, I woke up! That big, loud alarm clock went off in my life and I realized that if I wanted the love I requested from others I had to love myself from the inside out in order to attract my heart's desires. It was a long journey but I took that exit waiting for me and today I without hesitation or question I know what I deserve and refuse to accept anything less than that.

Finding the love of your life is your right but it is your birthright to be the love you desire and experience love at a Divine level. Whether you are single, married, divorced or in a relationship focus your energy on loving yourself first. Spend a lot of time showing yourself compassion, recognizing how spectacular you are, approving of yourself just as you are and being gentle and affectionate toward yourself. When you are intentional about this and successful at it the love you desire will be reflected out into the world and that which is like you will be attracted to you. Don't be afraid to look deep within no matter what your past story is. Today you have a new canvas and a new pen to create the love you want for yourself and your life partner.

Christine's story may inspire you to courageously love yourself and attract the love of your life.

LET GO OF FEAR AND LET LOVE IN

Christine Pembleton's Story

When I was getting ready for my first date with Bob, my husband of five years, I was scared out of my mind. Sure, I had been on numerous dates before but I felt something different— something I'd never experienced before. What I felt was a mixture of things. On the one hand, I knew he was everything I'd wanted in a husband and life partner. And then there was a slight fear that what I'd always wanted would not want me. I was afraid that after all this time of dating and searching that I would once again be disappointed by what I thought was best for me. And even though I was afraid, I knew that I had to still go. Needless to say, the date was magical—better than I could have hoped for in my life. If I hadn't have gone, if I'd cancelled or postponed that night, who knows what might have happened.

Now that I'm a relationship coach, it always amazes me that my clients are more afraid of having what they want then not having it at all. Many people are afraid that if they met 'the one', the relationship wouldn't last or they would somehow mess it up. That fear keeps them from dating, making commitments or being confident in their love life. And I understand that fear and power it can hold on you if you don't know how to overcome it. What I've learned about fear is that we can overcome it. Whatever situation we fear, if we experience it fully, we are no longer bound to its hold on our lives.

For me, it was going on a date that I instinctively knew would change my life. For you, it could be opening yourself up to love, saying yes to a persistent suitor, or agreeing to marry your long-term love. Whatever fear may be looming in your life, just know that you have a choice in how you operate in your life. You could decide to live in fear or decide to overcome it. It's your choice, either way. As for me, I'm glad I took the plunge. It was an emotional roller coaster at times, but it was so worth it. I hope you'll take the plunge as well, and see how amazing life can be when fear can no longer hold you.

—*Christine Pembleton,*
Companion Coach and Author
www.readytobeawife.com

Christine speaks about "instinctively going on a date that would change her life" despite her fears. She didn't allow her inner critic to talk her out of a potential experience of a life time that would eventually open the door to a soul union with her life partner. The beauty in Christine's story is that she chose to tell fear to get out so love could rush in. If you reflect back on her story you'll see her inner critic and old fear stories attempted to trick her out of her treat. The old negative mental tape of "what I want may not want me" tried to play on repeat and Christine said, "no, not today, not this guy" and she boldly stepped into the power of saying yes; yes to love for herself and yes to allowing someone to give her the love she deserved.

When Christine said yes, she said "yes I am worthy, I have value and I deserve to have a loving man in my life."

I applaud her bravery and cheer you on as you step into the power of yes. How often are you saying no to loving you? How often are you saying no to approving of yourself, accepting who you are and recognizing your greatness with gentle compassion? A better set of questions might be how are you saying yes to fearing love, settling for less, and or taking what you can get? There are reasons why you are accepting this kind of love in your life and only you know the answers. Regardless of what your relationship status is the following questions may inspire the answers within to rise to the surface you can address them.

Love Reflection Questions

What kinds of stories are in your past love chapters?

What have you learned about love from your family stories?

What mental love tapes are on continuous play in your mind?

What kind of love relationship do you have with yourself?

Are you cultivating love from the inside out or seeking love from the outside in, how and why?

What fears do you have about loving yourself and receiving love?

My hope for you is that some answers, thoughts and or feelings about your ability to love yourself came up. If you answered the questions honestly you should see that it's all about you and the choices you are making in your life about love. In every second of your life you are consciously or subconsciously choosing how to think, feel and behave. You are choosing whether you will attract or repel love. You are choosing whether you are worth of love and how you will accept or deny it. You are choosing to author the story of your life with love or fear.

When you finally realize that love is a powerful energy source and embrace it your life will dramatically transform. When authentic love is alive within you everything else within you comes to life. Your Geni(us) is awakened and ready to grant your wishes. Your SHero is on standby waiting for your lead and command. Things you are passionate about are your pulse for living. You bravely stare fear in the face and say bring it on! When love is raging within your dreams leap off the shelf and become a reality. When you think, feel and behave in a loving manner doors open up, you experience more joy, you feel alive inside and the possibilities are endless. Think about it, when you do things that make you happy and bring satisfaction it's because you love them. When you are doing work you love your life feels more rewarding. When you spend time with people you love you feel appreciated and inspired. When you are actively creating your dream life you are intentionally including all the things you love. The opposite is true when you live in fear. Fear smothers joy, passion, excitement, and fulfillment and as it has been said fear and love cannot exist in the same mindset. You are not able to "feel" the results of love when you "think" in fear.

This is true for all your relationships whether personal or professional. I guarantee you will experience more pleasure, passion and purpose when you begin to think, feel and behave lovingly in all of your relationships. The relationship you have with yourself sets the standard for all other relationships so set the bar high. Believe you deserve the best, accept the best, be your best and give your best to those who deserve it. If you desire to experience the sweetness of life, move towards love. If you desire to have a fulfilling career, move towards love. If you desire to be authentic in every moment, move towards love. For every step you take towards love and with love all the components of your life will expand and fill your heart with more peace and joy. Be fearless, be courageous start a new love affair with yourself right now in this moment. Make it a point to take daily sips of the powerful energy source, the super-juice; self-love.

Daily Sips of Self-Love

- Forgive yourself for all the unhealthy thoughts, feelings, behaviors and choices you've made in the past.
- Forgive those who have hurt you or caused you pain; set yourself and them free.
- Set standards for your life and honor them by living them and teaching other people how to respect and honor them as well.
- Accept your limitations and celebrate your strengths.
- Work towards creating inner peace by accepting who you are instead of pursuing perfection.
- Feed your mind, body and spirit by with healthy things they crave.
- Use the past chapters of your life as a springboard to achieve your goals, dreams and desires.
- Remove the toxic people from your life and surround yourself with positive and supportive people.
- Determine and live by your core values and refuse to compromise them.
- Make a list of all the things you love to do, the things that make you smile and bring you joy and do them.
- Take time everyday to pray, meditate and envision how you want to be in life.
- Read books that inspire you, empower your life and equip you with strategies for living and loving your life.
- Only say yes to the things that serve your highest good. Say yes when you mean yes and no when you mean no.
- Don't take on tasks and projects out of fear or obligation.

- Discover what you are passionate about and turn it into your purpose for living.
- Stop working a job and create a career to do work you love.
- Share your gifts by volunteering for a program or cause you believe in.
- Take time to journal your ideas, goals, dreams and desires and be sure to write down things that you are grateful for.
- Spend time with people you admire or those who inspire you.
- Invest your time, energy and money into personal development programs.
- Seek out a mentor, someone who is living the life you desire and learn how they achieved and maintain their life success.
- Hire a personal or professional coach to help you go from where you are to where you want to be.
- Make it a point at least once a day to remind yourself how wonderful, wise, and brilliant you are.
- Intentionally speak love in your mind, allow love to be a daily part of your life and never be afraid to love yourself first; you deserve it.

"You either move toward something you love or away from something you fear. The first expands. The second constricts."

—*Tom Crum*

TEN
LET YOUR SHERO SHINE

*T*HERE COMES A DEFINING MOMENT WHERE YOU FINALLY REALIZE THAT YOU MUST PUT YOURSELF FIRST IN LIFE, LOVE AND CAREER. UNTIL THIS MOMENT OCCURS, YOU WILL CONTINUE TO WATCH YOUR LIFE BE CREATED ON SOMEONE ELSE'S CANVAS WITH THEIR VISION IN MIND. YOUR LIFE STORY WILL BE WRITTEN WITH SOMEONE ELSE'S PEN AND THE ENDING WILL BE FILLED WITH MANY REGRETS.

Now let me explain. I don't mean that "it's all about you" in a vain, selfish way with no regard to other people. What I mean is, it is your birthright to dream your own dream, to write your own story and to make your physical, mental and spiritual needs a priority in your life. It is your birthright to live a peaceful, joy-filled abundant life. It is your birthright to wake up loving your life and show up in the world as a bright light that illuminates the lives of others. You see, when you take care of you, dream your dream and write your own story you inspire and empower others to do the same.

Taking care of you and putting yourself at the top of your life list is actually a double gift; a wonderful gift to yourself and others. When you are at peace you create peace in the lives of others. When you are filled with joy, you bring light to those in darkness. When you are happy you attract more happiness into your life. When you take responsibility for creating your life you model the importance of owning your personal power for others. The end result is that your ownership allows you to make it all about them (friends, family, colleagues and clients) without losing or sacrificing yourself. I don't know about you but I think that is a beautiful, magical moment where no one loses and you create a win-win for you and the people you engage with. Who doesn't want to win?

The winning I speak of is you fully embracing and stepping into your inner shine. You may not believe it or are unsure of it but there is a bright light within you. How do I know, because you were born with it, it's a part of your divine DNA. Over time life circumstances, events, relationships and experiences may have dimmed it but it's there and as you travel this journey of fear-free living it will slowly be revitalized. Have you ever looked at a picture of yourself and wondered who that woman in the picture is? You know that picture where you may look unhappy, dull and lacking the luster of life? If so, what you are seeing is a light that is barely flickering and fighting to stay alive. It's usually a photo that you don't like looking at and or refuse to share with others. I bet you've also seen a fabulous photo of yourself where you look alive, vibrant and joyful. That photo is a reflection of your inner shine bursting through so strongly that you feel the energy vibrations of self-love and joy. The depictions in each of those photos are an example of how you show up in the world. When your inner light is glowing brightly your presence is recognized by others and you feel luminous from the inside out. The same is true when you feel dark and dull on the inside that is how you show up in the world even when you attempt to put on a joyful mask.

My goal in this chapter is to help you learn how to master the inner game of authentic brilliance. No mask, disguise or façade can cover up the discomfort and dis-ease you feel on the inside. Showing up in the world this way is exhausting, incongruent, unfulfilling and really dishonors your value and self-worth. I'm not expecting you to mimic anyone but who you are in your core. I'm not expecting you to live up to someone else's definition of "shining." I am not expecting you to show up like the glamorous divas you may see in the media. My hope is that you will define what shine means to you and find the clarity, confidence and courage to simply show up as your best self. I've had the opportunity to coach many women on defining and living in their shine and I must say it's truly remarkable to see the metamorphosis take place. That's what I desire for you.

My friend Christina experienced her inner shine transformation and her life has been one thrilling, rewarding and fulfilling adventure ever since. Read her story and discover how defining, embracing and revealing her shine is inspiring other women to simply let their SHero shine!

WHAT I LEARNED FROM BRITNEY SPEARS

Christina Morassi's Story

In my twenties, I started out my career in the glamorous world of fashion photography in New York City. I worked as a photo assistant for some of the best photographers in the world on shoots with Giselle, Heidi Klum, and Paris Hilton. Part of my job was the oh-so-humbling experience of being a stand-in for these supermodels and celebrities. Once we would find the location, set up the lights, and have everything else in place, the photo assistant would then step in to have their picture taken so that the photographer could see how the lighting looked. Inevitably I would be dressed in work clothes, deep in work mode, and not exactly looking my best. It was quite the daily experience to see a picture of myself, side-by-side with a picture of an uber celebrity after hours of hair and makeup, and wearing designer clothes.

I knew I had to find a way to meet this situation head-on. This is what happened. One day I was on a shoot with Britney Spears for a major advertising campaign. As I set up the lights, she walked on set and while she was nice enough, she was tiny and seemed like a normal person. Well, when the photographer picked up his camera and pressed that first shutter, WOW! Britney Spears turned it 'on' like I have never seen another human being do before. It was as if someone had flipped a giant light switch, and a comet streaked through the studio emitting high wattages of golden light. It was then that I understood her broad mass appeal. She literally had found a way to turn on her brilliance and 'SHINE'.

I learned from Britney that day. The next time I had my picture taken as a stand-in I tried my best to flip on my own 'switch'. I looked for ways to turn on my own shine from within. I attempted to communicate my own inner brilliance to the camera. It was a wild experiment! Sometimes it worked and sometimes my eyes were just plain dead in the photo. However, I learned from every single picture. Eventually, I got so savvy that I turned into a bit of a ham, and became renowned as the assistant who turned it on for stand-in photos. One photographer even talked about someday making a book of the myriad of fun Polaroids we had created! It was amazing how far I had come and I owe it all to Britney Spears.

Flash forward a few years...

After questioning the fashion photography world, I left New York City and moved to Los Angeles on a whim. For the next 10 years I jumped into the healing arts and studied incredible modalities such as Craniosacral Therapy, Polarity Therapy, Shamanic work, Reiki, and massage. I was learning about a whole different kind of shine. This one came from healing, living in authenticity, and sharing your gifts with the world. I never forgot what I learned from Britney. Even though I had let go of photography for 8 years, I got curious about how I might bring the transformation work and photography together as one. Last year I finally launched my business as a business coach who uses photography as a shamanic tool in my practice. Now, I get to help all of my clients learn how to shine like Britney.

So in closing, I want you to know that shining brightly is merely about flipping a switch, and we all have one! It doesn't matter how scary it is for you to be seen, be visible, and shine. You only need to practice in small ways that build up over time. For me, it wasn't something that I grew up knowing how to do either. I learned from Britney, and eventually exercised that muscle enough to become my own comet in photos and in life. You can too.

—*Christina Morassi,*
Roaring Business Coach & Shamanic Photographer
http://christinamorassi.com/

Now that's a brave and fearless woman! In the midst of super models and celebrities, Christina found the courage to embrace her shine switch and flip it. It's one thing to acknowledge that you have a shine but flipping the switch and showing up luminous is a whole new level of fearlessness. I love Christina's story because I've had the opportunity to virtually watch her light become brighter and brighter over the past year. Christina doesn't know it but ever since we've become virtually acquainted I've noticed her standing firm in her brilliance and because she was brave enough to flip her switch women are attracted to her like a ship to a lighthouse. They see and feel the power of her shine presence and openly or secretly say "I want and deserve that kind of life and way of being too." This has created a huge shift in the way Christina lives her life, conducts business, attracts clients and shows up in the world. What a perfect example of "being the change you want to see in the world."

Before you begin your work on shining in life you must define what shine looks and feels like in your life. Think back on those moments when you felt alive, excited, fulfilled, confident and bold. What were you thinking and feeling? Who were you with and what were you doing? How were you physically and spiritually showing up in the world? That's the shine I want you to re-discover and define for you. Go back to those moments when you felt like you were on top of the world, all was well and you felt fantastic about your life. Take a few minutes to write down your definition of you want to shine in the world.

Shine Reflection Questions

When I reflect on those moments... I had these kinds of thoughts:

When I reflect on those moments... I felt like this.

When I had those kinds of moments I was doing this.

When I had those kinds of moments I spent time
with these people.

When I had those kinds of moments I was doing this
in my life.

My definition of shining is...

In Christina's story, she talked about a "different kind of
shine, the kind that comes from healing, living in authenticity,
and sharing your gifts with the world." She put in the effort
to learn, grow and enhance who she was from the inside out.
She realized the significance in personal development and
investing in herself. When the time came to flip the switch her
light showed up like a luminous comet, undeniably present
and brilliant. I'm confident that Christina in her journey
towards shining took many risks. I'll even go out on a limb
and say she risked failure, looking silly, being misunderstood
and a long list of other risks. She was brave enough to define

her own shine and show up and show out; not like Britney but as her authentic self.

When you choose to show up and shine in your life there are some risks to consider and some benefits to be experienced. Christina used her fears as fuel for her dreams; what a wise choice she made. Did you know you can use your fear to fuel your dreams? Fear is energy and you can either allow that energy to propel you forward or paralyze your personal progress. There are risks you'll need to take to let your SHero shine through. Some risks will need to be taken without over thinking the choice and others can be calculated and intentional. I bet you've thought about taking some risks and I also bet that your inner-critic talked you out them or convinced you to do it later. That's the inner critic functioning at optimum performance; its number one goal is to talk you out of living your life with courage. So let's bring those fears to the surface so you can face them. When you think about taking risks in your life how would you respond to the following statements?

What risks do you desire or need to take?

Why do you desire or need to take these risks?

What are the potential setbacks or side effects of taking these risks?

What fears keep you from taking the risks?

What are the rewards or benefits of taking these risks?

Do you have more to lose or gain by taking these risks?

Will taking these risks liberate and enhance your life or paralyze it and place it on pause?

These statements or questions are not just to make you think; they are useful, strategic and allow you to take calculated risks. Calculated risks provide you with the opportunity to weigh your options before you take a step towards a desire. When you define shining on your own terms you should not fear taking the risk to shine because you cannot fail when you set the rules. When you live up to your own standards in life your success is measured by your perception of yourself and your ability to succeed.

Allowing your SHero to shine is a beautiful thing. When you define your shine there is less pressure, competition and the agony of comparing yourself to others dramatically decreases. Shining is about loving yourself from the inside out, showing up in the world as your authentic self and living the ease and grace of knowing you are fabulous just the way you are.

Shining is not about being flamboyant, arrogant and egotistical yet it's about finding that special light inside of you and not being afraid to show it to the world. There are more than a million stars in the Universe and regardless of the size, location and position of each star they do what they were created to do, shine. You are a star in the Universe and you too were created to shine in your own way. Don't fear shining, it is your birthright and when you shine you light up the world and give hope to those who need to find their shine. Simply put, shining means you step into the world and live, love, and work as your best self. This is your moment. It's time for you to shine and do it fearlessly.

"It's not because things are difficult that we dare not venture. It's because we dare not venture that they are difficult."

—*Seneca*

THE COURAGE
TO CREATE PROSPERITY

*I*F YOU COULD SNAP YOUR FINGERS AND HAVE WHATEVER YOU WANTED, WHAT WOULD IT BE? WOULD YOU CHOOSE LOVE, JOY, FAME, SUCCESS, HEALTH, VITALITY AND OR MONEY? WOULD YOU CHOOSE TRAVELING, A FINISHED PUBLISHED BOOK, FAMILY HARMONY AND OR A SUCCESSFUL CAREER? IF I COULD BE SO BOLD TO MAKE A SUGGESTION, I WOULD CHOOSE PROSPERITY FOR YOU. WHY PROSPERITY YOU MAY BE WONDERING?

Prosperity is so much more than wealth, a fat bank account and or being rich. Prosperity is an abundance of many things such as love, success, and peace and yes money. Prosperity is a flourishing, thriving condition; a state of abundance and success. The definition of prosperity only provides you with a skeleton of what prosperity really is because it's up to you to put the meat on those bones. Many people have fears about money and financial prosperity, I know, I've had my fair share of fears that kept me from attracting, receiving and giving money. Quite frankly, this is one very deeply rooted and often subconscious fear that still creeps into my mind.

My money story is being re-written as you read this. The old mental tapes are being erased and I have begun a soul journey to discover what my soul imprints have stored regarding money and prosperity. You can say all the affirmations you want and take all the prosperity courses out there but if you have money fears deeply imbedded in your soul and spirit there is great work to be done at a cellular level. I had no idea money or lack thereof ran that deep until I met some marvelous spirit coaches who helped me tap into this unknown territory.

My prosperity awakening began just a short time ago. I had always been ambitious, driven and goal-oriented. I grew up in a poor family and was raised on public assistance so I knew the pain and the blessing of living monetarily poor. I watched my mother "steal from Paul to pay Peter, rub two nickels together and make a dollar, and brilliantly use her God-given talents of sewing, fashion and crafts to provide and make ends meet. She is a resilient and resourceful woman who knew how move through the struggle with quite a bit of ease and grace. I also knew what "lack" looked like and felt like and somewhere along the way vowed to never be in that position when I grew up. This is a part of my money story.

My money story continued with a personal super-charged drive to evolve, elevate and advance in every area possible. I realized higher education; something my mother and grandmother didn't have the luxury to afford was my golden ticket out of poverty. I wasn't necessarily running towards prosperity or wealth but running away from lack. Little did I know lack dug its paralyzing paws deep into the fiber of my being. My money story is generations of scarcity, financial struggle and lack of financial prosperity. Most of the education or enlightenment, primarily passed down by the women in my family. The women in my family were miracle workers, faithful servants and SHeroes rich with love, laughter and sass! I am grateful for each one of them, and what they taught me about money; it doesn't define who you are and it can't buy happiness.

My educational background is an eclectic one. After high school I graduated from beauty school, worked in a few salons, enjoyed it yet there was that tug in my spirit to be free, in charge, in control; an entrepreneur. I opened my first salon and business in the basement of my grandmother's house and had some success but soon realized that was not my calling. I then graduated from nursing school in 1997 and worked as a nurse for a year or so making good money. My original nursing goal was to work as a OB/GYN nurse, and I soon discovered it was every other nurse's goal too, so the waiting list was long. I decided I wanted to help people in a bigger way and make a difference in the world. I enrolled in undergraduate school and completed a Bachelor's degree in Criminal Justice. This was a very fulfilling field to work in as it allowed me wonderful, life-changing opportunities to work with at-risk youth, families and women experiencing domestic violence. I was paid well, enjoyed my work and pretty content in life but there was still something, a void that needed to be filled. While I desired to make more money I craved meaningful work as well.

I had the opportunity to work at a domestic violence shelter working with women and children escaping various forms of violence. I took the job as an Americorps volunteer, worked forty hours a week and was paid a meager stipend of about three-hundred dollars a month. This was a soul-enlightening moment; a moment when I realized money wasn't everything and that doing work you love and serving the world was a form of prosperity. Sure it created some economic challenges but I could feel the void being filled. I thoroughly enjoyed every moment of this job especially the opportunity to conduct individual and group counseling sessions and the community education component which involved public speaking. Two fires were ignited within me and I realized how much I enjoyed counseling and speaking.

I became fully aware of my ability to connect, relate, comfort and advise people. As a teenager I was the friend many of my friends came to for advice and support. I wondered what it was about me that made them think I had the answers and ironically often times I did. I decided to capitalize on this God-gift and enrolled in a graduate program and eventually graduated (on the Dean's List) from college and earned a Master's degree in Counseling. I went on to provide professional counseling in various settings working with youth and families and my income increased with every opportunity.

After many advancements, promotions, recognition and two layoffs in a row, another awakening occurred. I wanted to be in control of my economic status and personal and financial prosperity. Fast forward three years later I ventured off into the unknown territory of entrepreneurship. This is the part of my story where my biggest fears about money are faced and conquered. Long story short, I learned I am the money, I can either attract or repel money and until my money story is re-written and my soul imprints are healed the abundance of money would elude me or the lack of money would consume me.

I am making peace with my money story. I am embracing and re-writing my money story and I am re-constructing my thoughts, beliefs and feelings about money. This book was actually put on hold for six months due to the peaks and valleys in my money story. On this journey of creating real prosperity I have learned many things about myself and how money or lack there of has become a silent but big part of who I am as I write this book. The beautiful thing is this story I've shared with you is not who I am deep in my core nor is it who I am becoming. I can honestly say my fears about money had more to do with the fear of success rather than the fear of failure. I had proved many times over that I could do anything I set my mind to.

Having a lot of money is one sign of business success in my opinion. Being prosperous in mind, body and spirit is the true definition of prosperity in general but I have learned it is okay to be blessed financially and that my blessing allows me to be a blessing to others. While I still have work to do in my money story I believe I deserve it, I am worthy of it and I can co-create it with intentional thoughts and actions, gratitude and a complete healing and re-writing of my story. I'm excited to share with you "I've come a long way, baby" and that prosperity is my birthright as it is yours.

Fear of not having enough or having too much money is real for many people. No matter what amount of money you need or desire if you are anything like me and most people your thoughts and feelings about money will either bring you an abundance of money or keep you in a state of lack and scarcity. You may be thinking, who wouldn't want to be wealthy? Read Amethyst's story and see if she can shed some light on the question.

WOULDN'T WANNA BE WEALTHY!

Amethyst Wyldfyre's Story

Faulty perceptions and mistaken judgments are a powerful combo for co-creating fear and self-limiting beliefs in a person. When they originate (as they often do) in childhood experiences that are far from memory when we become adults it can be quite a challenge to uncover and heal them so that we can live the life we were born to live and fulfill our true destiny.

Fear of wealth was never one of the fears I had any conscious awareness of until *many* of the other fears that were embedded in my soul had finally been surfaced and cleared. This clearing created an opening for me to go deeper and wider in my exploration of what was blocking the way to the life of my dreams. When I dove in to the ocean of my soul once again to explore the core—what surfaced for me around wealth was a surprise—a painful—very painful memory of my early adolescent years. I was gangly, a tall skinny girl with glasses and big feet and my mother dressed me in clothes that were more attuned to the 50's than the 70's. It was bad enough to look weird what was worse was I was constantly followed by a group of girls who would go around the school yard taunting me unmercifully not only about my clothes but also about my "rich" Daddy who always had a new car. What these girls didn't know was my family wasn't rich—we were comfortable smack dab in the middle class but far from rich—my dad had a new car every few weeks because he was a car salesman. Right then I think Wound #1 was formed around having money. *If you have money people will torture you*—was seeded into my soul.

Wound #2 happened when I was just getting out of high school and was the result of my mother's projections and stories about what happened to my dad when his company was bought out. He lost his job when the new owner's took over—the new owner being someone who had been one of his employees previously— and according to my mother's story—betrayed my father who had been the one to promote this guy from the ranks. This situation caused Wound #2 and I believed that *If you are wealthy, you screw over and mistreat the people who helped you get to the top.*

Fast forward to my mid 20's when I was working for a man who had, what was to me at the time, a lot of money. He was a wealthy multimillionaire real estate developer and owner of several apartment complexes and office buildings. He was not *super* rich but certainly among the affluent. This man treated me well in a lot of ways. He was a good mentor and provided me with both an education on the job and academically; but he was also a mean, angry, and arrogant man who used to berate service people and scream at his stock broker on a daily basis. Working with him was like sitting next to a volcano most of the time and often after he'd blow I'd be following up behind him apologizing profusely to the people he'd abused verbally when he wasn't getting his way. My experiences with him created Wound #3: *People who are wealthy are mean, arrogant, explosively angry, self-centered bullies.*

The beauty of surfacing these stories is now there is awareness. With consciousness and a handy tool that I often use when working with my clients called Rewriting Contracts, I was able to go in to a negotiation with my soul and come to a place of having a new agreement for myself around wealth. My new contract is: *"It is safe and healthy to be wealthy."*

Since shifting into this new contract I've discovered I'm much more content with and grateful for what I have already in my life. All that I need and desire is right here. I've got a beautiful home, a lovely and loving child, a wonderful pet, an amazing business partner, a Divine business through which I serve some incredibly talented and passionate clients and enough resources, ideas, and phenomenal connections to take my life to the next level and really serve with even more abandon than ever before. I am wonderfully wealthy in every way!

Because I work with energy I believe the different ways we look at and think about money have different frequencies or energies. This is why some people have money issues all the time. Others may have plenty of money come in and go out and are in a state of relative abundance most of the time, and others are able to really create, manage and generatively channel wealth. What I've discovered in my own healing journey is wealth is much more than accumulating a pile of money. To be truly wealthy one must first acknowledge one's worthiness to be wealthy. This is an inner game that requires a lot of introspection, exploration, and often a skilled facilitator or navigator to probe those depths and surface the experiences, beliefs and fears that are hidden in the dark. When we do this inner work we discover our own value, our own gifts and our own personal connection with the source of all that is and from which true wealth springs eternal. When we are tapped in to that source, through our own deep heart connection with our true nature then we are blessed with a wealth of wisdom, experience, gifts, talents, and surprise abilities and resources of strength and courage that we wouldn't know of otherwise. From this place of acknowledgment of our own innate divinity we can create wealth beyond measure and we have the power and the capacity to leave behind a legacy of good that lives and serves beyond our life time. This is divine wealth. This is our true destiny.

—*Amethyst Wyldfyre,*
Energy Mastery Mentor
http://www.theenergyjourney.com

Amethyst's story speaks to more than just money. Her story is really a testimony of how healing and doing the work from the inside out is essential for creating and living the life you desire. It takes courage to embrace, own and re-create your money story and the other pieces of your unique life story. As previously stated, prosperity is an abundance of many things such as love, success, peace and yes money. Prosperity is a flourishing, thriving condition; a state of abundance and success. Money is simply energy and when you learn how to channel that energy from a divine source of abundance you can create financial prosperity and other forms of prosperity in your life.

I once feared prosperity until I realized how prosperity allows me to serve the world in a bigger way. Now when I think about money I envision how many people I can serve, inspire and empower with the financial resources of my prosperity. I think about how much I can give to the world with an abundance of money. I think about how I am creating a new money story and creating an abundance legacy for my son and his children. As my prosperity continues to increase I am mindful to remind myself that I am worthy of prosperity.

You are worthy of prosperity. Amethyst illustrates this wonderfully in her story. While your initial thoughts and feelings about financial prosperity may be centered around your needs and desires, financial abundance blesses more than just your life and your family's life it serves the world in a beautiful way. If you are struggling financially you must return to your source, your core, your spirit and examine the fears that keep abundance from filling your life. If you see having an abundance of money as a negative or evil thing, I challenge you to see how you can serve and uplift humanity with financial prosperity. If you desire more money in your life you must go deeper than your thoughts and feelings about money. You will need to experience a profound shift in the energy vibrations you send out into the world related to money. The best way to illustrate this is to envision the ripple effect. If you toss a pebble into a pond it will create ripples in the water and they will expand out at a certain pace and distance. Those ripples are like energy vibrations or the deep cellular, soul waves you send out from you spirit. The pace and distance of those ripples increases when you toss a brick into the pond thus sending a stronger, bigger vibration into the water.

The pebble scenario serves as an example of limiting beliefs, small thinking and little amounts of worthiness. The brick scenario serves as an example of deep seated positive beliefs, bigger thinking and larger amounts of worthiness. If you are "the brick" you are energetically casting out stronger, bigger, more believable soul vibrations that you deserve what you desire, seek and ask for. It is not enough to say you want prosperity, to think prosperous thoughts, and or to feel prosperous feelings. If you really want prosperity you have to believe you deserve in the depths of your soul, you have feel it deep in your bones, you have to know without a shadow of a doubt in your heart that you are worthy and you have to combine all of those actions into one powerful projection of energy. This combination becomes the brick (vibration) you toss in the pond and the pond (Universe) has no choice but to respond by expanding in pace (how fast money comes) and distance (how much money you have and how many people you serve with it).

It's time to make peace with your past money story and create a new story of prosperity. It's time to move from pebble thinking and become the brick that vibrates far and wide. It's time bring forth your fears about money and get to the source of their existence. It is time to make the transition from lack to abundance. As with every other part of your life, living an abundant prosperous life is a choice. When it's all said and done you can release your prosperity Genie at any moment, face your fears about money and other forms of prosperity and through love and gratitude you can intentionally create a prosperous life. I encourage you to stretch every fiber of your energetic being and move from sabotaging your prosperity to allowing it to flow with ease and grace. When you define prosperity on your own terms you choose how wealthy you are. If you stop and really look at your life you have much to be grateful for thus you are already prosperous. That knowing deep in your core is the magical fuel to creating new levels of abundance and prosperity. If that is what you desire, be courageous enough to do the work from the inside out to achieve and receive the desires of your heat. Don't allow your fears to block your blessings and the blessings you can create for those you love and the world. Your true prosperity lives in your soul.

"Self-sabotage is when we say we want something and then go about making sure it doesn't happen."

—*Alyce P. Cornyn-Selby*

TWELVE
Mastering Your Mindset... Creating Magic

*N*EXT TO YOUR SOUL YOUR MIND IS THE MOST BEAUTIFUL PART OF YOUR BEING. OUR MINDS HAVE THE EXTRAORDINARY CAPACITY TO CREATE ANYTHING WE DESIRE. YOU CAN TRULY CREATE MAGICAL MOMENTS IN YOUR LIFE WITH YOUR BEAUTIFUL MIND WHEN YOU LEARN TO MASTER YOUR MINDSET. THERE ARE NO LIMITS TO WHAT YOU CAN BECOME, DO, HAVE AND EXPERIENCE WHEN YOU MASTER *THE ART OF FEAR-FREE LIVING* AND AWAKEN THE GENI(US) WITHIN YOU. JUST LIKE THE GENIE IN A BOTTLE YOU HAVE THE MAGICAL POWER TO GRANT YOURSELF THE WISHES OF YOUR HEART. THE SWEET BONUS IS YOU HAVE THE PERSONAL POWER TO GRANT MORE THAN JUST THREE. DO YOU REALIZE THE LIMITLESS POSSIBILITIES YOU CAN CREATE WITH THE POWER OF YOUR MIND?

I get all excited and tingly inside when I simply think of what I can create, what you can create and what we can create when we choose the become the masters of our minds. When you are mindful you can create magical miracles. Mindfulness, simply put, is one's ability to be and live in the moment. It means to be emotionally, spiritually and physically present in every situation. When you live in fear,

173

you often escape and avoid being in the moment. When you are mindful, you are in control of your thoughts, feelings, emotions and actions. When you are mindful you are tuned into what you want, need and or desire in your life. When you are mindful you are awakened in life instead of living on auto-pilot. When you are mindful you are staring fear in the face instead of running from your fears.

The essence, the key, the secret to Mastering *The Art of Fear-Free Living* is all about being mindful. When you are mindful you are listening to your inner critic but not reacting to it. When you are mindful you actively practice opposite action to quiet your inner critic. When you are mindful you are not blaming other people for the quality of your life yet you are taking responsibility for creating the life you desire. If you are struggling with what mindfulness looks and feels like in real life here are a few examples.

Mindfulness in real life looks like this:

- You are paying attention to your thoughts and adjusting them from negative to positive as they occur.
- You feel your feelings instead of ignoring them.
- You intentionally give mental energy to the things you desire.
- You focus on what you want instead of what you don't want.
- You listen to your heart and intuitive voice and let them guide your decisions.
- You use your core values as the compass for designing your fearless life.

- You are aware of when your emotional energy is being depleted and you take steps to restore it.
- You realize when certain people are toxic and you work to remove them from your life.
- You accept you have thinking errors and have worked to make them productive thoughts.
- You are always aware of your personal power and you use it to create your life instead of destroy it.

The above are just a few ways mindfulness shows up in your life. Mindfulness means you are in the driver's seat of your life and you are in control of your life by being present in each moment. As you continue on your journey of Mastering *The Art of Fear-Free Living*, be sure to incorporate these simple strategies for mindful living.

Simple Ways to Be Mindful

- Take time out every day to sit quietly and reflect upon your life.
- Set goals for each day and make sure they are goals you can achieve.
- Find time during each day to breathe deeply and or meditate.
- Always listen to that faint, quiet voice that always speaks the truth.
- Be authentic in every moment. Trying to be someone else creates stress, chaos and anxiety.
- Focus all your thoughts on what you want. If you focus on what you don't want, that's exactly what you will get.

- When you feel afraid don't run from the fear, face it and work through it.
- Pay attention to how your body is responding to certain situations. The body never lies. If you are experiencing physical symptoms such as fatigue, headaches, pain or other signs of stress you should address why the pain is there instead of treating the symptoms.
- When engaging with other people feel your feelings, monitor your thoughts and notice your behaviors. Adjust them in the moment to re-direct your energy.
- Don't give away your power by contemplating, worrying, arguing or stressing out about certain people and situations.
- Only make choices that take you towards your highest most spiritual place.
- Do what you love every day.
- Be selective about who you choose to be in your inner circle.
- Journal your thoughts and reflect back on them to monitor your progress.
- Listen to music and take time out to simply relax.

There are so many things you can do to be mindful. This list includes just a few things you can do to begin to practicing mindfulness every day.

Fear is a part of life. The inner critic will show up again. You will experience moments when you are afraid to take action. Life will change and the vision for your life will evolve. The most important thing to know is that mastering The *Art of Fear-Free Living* is not about eliminating your fears forever. It is a journey, it is a way of being and living your life. Living fear-free simply means that you have chosen to not let fear captivate your life, hold your dreams hostage and keep you from experiencing the sweetness and beauty in life. Living fear-free allows you to show up in the world as your luminous authentic self with no shame, regret or guilt. Living fear-free deepens your sense of worthiness to receive love and prosperity. When you live a fear-free life you are fully awakened, mindful and your Geni(us) serves as your guide in life instead of your inner critic. The wonderful thing about living fear-free is your SHero, your champion your Genie is readily available and waiting for you to ask for what you want so it can be granted.

The magic in creating fearless living success lies in your power of choice. Remember you can choose how you respond to fear (not react). Be awakened in every moment. Listen to your wise voice. Choose in each moment to face your fears instead of running from them. You will need people to support you on this journey. Begin now developing your "dream team." This is a small group of people who believe in you and your dreams and will support you in making your dream a reality. Be careful who you choose. Be sure to choose people who are already where you are trying to go. Choose people who are on their own journey of fearless living. Choose people who will hold you accountable and keep you on track. Choose people who will celebrate you and your success.

While you are an amazing woman who can stand boldly in your personal power the real power lies in creating a community to support you and sharing space with other fearless and fabulous women. I believe there is truth in the notion that the quality of your life will be the result of the six people you spend the most time with. Be wise and discerning and allow your Geni(us) to help you choose who should be in your inner circle. The beautiful thing is it's your life and how it plays out in your manuscript and in reality is totally up to you.

I love Nike's slogan "Just Do It." While it may be challenging it must be done and you can either do it with struggle and strife or you can do it with ease and grace. Do it on your own terms, do it at your own pace, do it by your rules it doesn't matter, just do it! Do what you may ask? It is whatever you decide it is. It is creating and living a fearless life. It is mastering *The Art of Fear-Free Living*; living a life where fear is welcomed, acknowledged, embraced, faced and conquered. A life where fear is used as an opportunity to learn, grow, evolve and transform from the inside out. A life where fear serves as the fuel to ignite your dreams and make your passions sizzle. A life where fear does not reign, yet your SHero courageously steps into the flow of your life and creates the ease and grace only she can.

There are no limits to what your mind can create. A mind is a terrible thing to waste. Choose today to not waste your mind on worry, doubt, guilt, shame, regret or fear. If you can conceive in your mind that you can be fearless and believe it with no doubt you can achieve it. Decide in this moment what you want to give your mental energy to and just do it! Don't over analyze it, don't contemplate it, don't procrastinate just decide how you want to think and begin thinking positive thoughts about you, others and the world. If you need to start slow that's okay. Pick one negative thought, turn it into a positive thought and think it as often as you can. Write it down, turn it into an affirmation and say it daily. When it's all said and done your real power lies in your mind. Your thoughts will either defeat you or release you. If you want to liberate your life and dreams think your way to freedom. No one is in control of your thoughts but you. The choice is yours; do you choose defeat or release? When you become the master of your mind you can create magic! Just do it!

"It's easier done than said."

—*Ellie Drake*

THIRTEEN

YOUR JOURNEY CONTINUES

OU NEED TO FORGIVE SOMEONE IN ORDER TO SET YOURSELF FREE AND THAT SOMEONE IS YOU. DON'T BE AFRAID TO LOOK WITHIN AND LET GO ALL THAT HOLDS YOUR LIFE CAPTIVE. YOU'LL ALWAYS HAVE FEARS, THE SECRET IS TO NOT LET THEM CONTROL THE CONTENT AND QUALITY OF YOUR LIFE. IF YOU ARE ABOUT TO GIVE UP AND THROW IN THE TOWEL FIND OUT WHAT YOU ARE AFRAID OF, EMBRACE IT, ACCEPT IT AND DEVISE A PLAN TO ELIMINATE THAT FEAR. IF YOU GIVE UP BEFORE YOU DO THIS, YOU'LL JUST HAVE TO FACE IT DOWN THE ROAD. AS YOU KNOW, FEAR IS FALSE-EVIDENCE-APPEARING-REAL INSTEAD OF FOCUSING ON FALSE EVIDENCE LOOK FOR TRUE EVIDENCE; YOUR SUCCESS, ACCOMPLISHMENTS, TRIUMPHS AND OTHER SITUATIONS WHERE YOU'VE SHOWN AND PROVED THAT YOU CAN, YOU WILL, AND YOU ARE COURAGEOUS.

Fear gives you the opportunity to show how strong, brave and wise you are. Choose to not allow fear to keep your life on layaway. Do everything with love and put your faith into action; this will help you reclaim your power and brilliantly in the world. Re-discover your light, let it shine and step into your SHero spotlight! Let your tests be your testimony and your mess be your message to the world that your story matters. When you fall down and get back up again you inspire the fallen to rise to their feet. When you honor, value and respect who you are so will the people in your life. When you stand up for what you believe in you give voice to the voiceless. When you show up in the world as your brilliant, powerful self you show others how to live in their Geni(us). You see, you may have thought this journey was about you and while it was to a certain extent it's much bigger than you could ever imagine. Your ability to find and release your courage is just one vibration in the universe designed to raise the courage vibration of women all over the world. When your SHero shows up in the world as loving beacon of light the sky has one more star in the darkness and the sun beams expand.

No matter where you are in your personal journey of freedom and liberation, know that you are right where you are supposed to be. There are no mistakes or coincidences. Everything that has happened to you is all a part of the plan no matter how painful it is or has been. The people in your life right now are there for a reason. Discover it, embrace it and get the lesson. The people who have left you their job is done, discover the lesson, learn from it and apply it to your life now. The people in transition waiting to join you on your journey are on their way in this moment. You may be in the beginning stages of the metamorphosis and it may feel like all hell is breaking loose. Stay on the journey. You may already be encapsulated in the tightly woven fibers of chrysalis, settle in, surrender and know you are about to experience some breakdowns. In this space don't struggle, don't fight it's not time for the breakthrough yet. This is the stage where you become enlightened, empowered and equipped to take flight. This is the moment when the real transformation takes place and your wings begin to bud. This is the moment where you take small steps in the dark knowing with full conviction and belief that your time to soar is just moments away. You may already be beyond this stage as you've received, learned and applied the lessons to your life. If you are here, it's time! It's time to gracefully push and stretch to break through the final layers of the cocoon. Your wings are fully developed, your beautiful soul colors are vibrant and your destination is ready for your arrival.

Gracefully push with love as your intention for all engagements. Speak lovingly to yourself. Give lovingly to others. Love yourself as you are. Do work you love and continue to paint and write your life with your love tools; optimism, compassion, forgiveness, intention, purpose, courage and authenticity. Every thought you think, feeling you feel and action you take anchored in love is the gentle force needed to breakthrough and break out. It's time for you to fly and soar above all pain, worry and doubt. You have everything you need and you've been provide with tools and strategies to equip you for the journey ahead. Don't be afraid of the metamorphosis. No matter how dark it seems or how much fear you may be experiencing, know that you are the Genie you've been waiting for. You are brave, wise and strong now put these tools in your back pack, summon your inner Geni(us), hop on your magic carpet and prepare to embark on a magical journey of courage and fearlessness.

I'm still on my journey and so are the extraordinary women you've read about. The journey never ends so pace yourself, enjoy the scenery, stop and smell the flowers and be authentic in every moment. Be mindful to live in a loving flow instead of living in fear and always allow your SHero to be your guide. You are not alone and if there is no one else walking this journey with you, God is with you, the 11 fearless women who shared their stories are with you and I am with you in spirit. On the next few pages you'll find affirmations for living a fear-free life and 50 Ways to Be More Fearless. Use these daily strategies and insights as inspiration and fuel for your mind, heart and spirit. Are you ready? Of course you are and so your journey continues...

As you approach the doorway to an authentic, fearless life you love take out your courage key, unlock the door and step into the light and on the path knowing deep in your soul that you are brave, brilliant powerful and resilient. Take a deep breath, believe in yourself, pop the top on that Genie bottle, and courageously create the magic you desire in your life.

"Be bold, be brave, and be courageous. It's time for you to master The Art of Fear-Free Living. *Do it now and do it afraid if you have to!"*

—*Catrice M. Jackson*

AFFIRMATIONS FOR LIVING A FEAR-FREE LIFE

- I am wise and seek what I need.
- I love freely without fear.
- I am not my past.
- It is safe for me to ask for what I need.
- I love myself and therefore I attract love.
- I am the author of my story.
- I deserve to have the desires of my heart.
- I have the power to transform my life.
- I listen to my Geni(us) she is always right.
- I know the questions and the answers I need.
- I can create peace in the midst of chaos.
- I see the light in every moment of darkness.
- I can only control my life.
- I choose to create opportunities instead of waiting for them.
- I am more powerful than fear.
- I deserve abundance, prosperity and wealth.
- I have the resources to conquer my fears.
- I am responsible for my thoughts, feelings and actions.
- I create my thoughts and therefore I create my now.
- I am a courageous champion.
- Fear does not control me.
- I create my definition of success and I am successful.
- It safe for me to speak my authentic voice.

- I can do anything I choose
- I radiate confidence in every moment.
- I am beautiful and I see the beauty in others.
- I release myself from fear, worry and doubt.
- I am fearless.

"Facing your fears is the doorway to freedom and courage is the key to unlocking your Genie."

—Catrice M. Jackson

Notes

Fear Post-Assessment

Please complete this assessment after reading this book. Use this scale (1-10) to rate your level of fear about the following issues.

Date of Assessment _____ Time _____

**10=Extreme Fear 8=Significant Fear 5=Moderate Fear
1= Very Little Fear 0= None**

____I worry about not having enough money to pay my bills

____I worry that I won't achieve my goals.

____I worry about people not supporting my dream.

____I worry that something bad is going to happen to me.

____I'm concerned that I may not have what it takes to be successful.

____I fear that others will talk about me if I take steps forward.

____I am afraid to fail.

____I fear that I am not good enough or that I don't deserve good things.

____I fear that my intimate relationship will not last.

____I'm afraid to dream.

____I am afraid I will lose my close relationships if I become successful.

____I fear success.

____I am afraid to die.

____I fear that I will lose my job.

___I am afraid to take risks.

___I am afraid my past will always haunt me.

___I am afraid to make mistakes.

___I fear the economic climate will keep me from having what I want.

___I fear that people are trying to undermine my success.

___I fear that my health will get worse.

___I'm afraid to quit my job and begin a career.

___I'm afraid to leave my relationship.

___I fear the unknown.

___I fear that God won't bless my life.

___I am afraid of my own power.

___I am afraid of just about everything.

*List your score here: _____

Regardless of your score, I hope you learned something new about yourself, were enlightened and feel more inspired to live fearlessly.

50 Ways
to Be More Fearless

1. Make a list of the things you need to forgive yourself
    for and one by one release the shame, guilt and regret.

2. Identify the people in your life you need to forgive.
    Choose to do the work within your heart to forgive them.

3. Start a courage journal and write down all the things you
    want to do and find creative ways to make them happen.

4. Decide what risks you can take now
    to be more courageous.

5. Remember the moments when you were wise and
    strong and how you were able to create success in
    those moments.

6. Make a list of the values and standards you want to
    live by and start living by them.

7. Think about all the things you do that you do not like
    or want to do and create your "not to do" list. Once
    the list is complete be brave and just stop doing them.

8. Use your fears to drive you towards your passion
    and purpose.

9. When you become aware of fear remember the
    awareness of fear is a signal that something in your life
    is missing.

10. See the see the significance of feeding your soul as you do in feeding your body. Determine how you will feed your soul every day.

11. Check your emotional energy tank and determine who is filling it or causing you to run on fumes. Determine what you can do to remove the energy stealers in your life and do it.

12. Decide what you can do every day to move from surviving in life to thriving in your life.

13. Every time you feel fearful, ask yourself this question "what is the worst that could happen if I do not face this fear and what is the worst that could happen if I do face this fear." You'll see you have more to lose by not facing your fears.

14. Remember you only have two choices in life. Be afraid and live afraid or be fearless and live fearless.

15. Instead of focusing your energy on your fears, focus your energy on how you can get the resources you need to conquer the fears.

16. Color the canvas of your life with vibrant, energetic, happy people who can keep you inspired to Master *The Art of Fear-Free Living.*

17. Remember that every day you have the choice to take down the old, dull and grey canvas and put up a blank one to create your fearless life.

18. Know that your personal power is like a big eraser. You have the power and choice to erase the negative thoughts about yourself. Erase the past hurts that are keeping you stuck. Erase everything in your life that is causing you distress and misery.

19. As you begin to create a fear free life, remember that you have the tools you need within you; you just have to seek them and use them.

20. Be mindful to stay off auto-pilot. Be sure to live fully awakened in each moment of your life.

21. Make it a personal priority to ask yourself every day "what do I need to face and how can I face it with the resources I need and do it with ease and grace.

22. Be intentional in every moment. Only engage in activities and conversations that move you one step closer to your goals.

23. Remember that facing your fears is simply about taking risks. You have to be willing to take some risks to get and experience what you desire.

24. Create a vision board and fill it up with words, pictures and quotes that depict how you want to live your fearless life.

25. Create your fearless life dream team. A small group of dedicated, positive, trustworthy people who believe in you and your dreams and will help you bring them to life.

26. Be mindful to not make excuses or reasons not to do something that can empower your life. Excuses are the doorway to failure.

27. When faced with a fear, instead of allowing yourself to worry and become paralyzed, seek out the resources to help you conquer the fear.

28. Be curious. When faced with a fear ask yourself this question "I wonder what would happen if I faced this fear." Be still and listen for the answer to come from your heart.

29. Make the choice to accept that you will have obstacles in your life and begin to see them as opportunities to strengthen your SHero.

30. Instead of dreading facing your fears, wake up each day with gratitude and ask yourself "how can I be brave today" and then take action.

31. Unsubscribe! That's right opt out of everything that does not fill your cup, fulfill you, serve your highest good and or take your one step closer to your highest self.

32. Surrender once a day. In the morning surrender to the Universe and let God order your steps. In the evening, surrender again and release all the toxicity you've taken in during the day.

33. Choose to be struggle free! Pay attention to the moments where there is struggle and decide in that moment that your life is not worth the pain and frustration that struggle brings.

34. Be accepting. Sometimes you've got to simply say "it is what it is" let it go and keep it moving.

35. Quit looking for the answers and choose to allow them to just come to you and enjoy life while you wait for the downloads to occur.

36. Trust yourself more. Trust that what you need will come. Trust that you know yourself better than anyone else. Stop fighting with your ShEgo and just trust yourself.

37. Take action! Worrying, contemplating, agonizing and analyzing are signs of struggle. Ask your heart, your soul whether you should act and if you feel peace overcome you then get out of your head and take action.

38. Learn how to filter out the background noise. The background noise is other people's opinions, demands and requests. It's your life do what you want to do and make your own decisions.

39. Release the need to be right or perfect. There's no such thing as perfect and you will never be right all the time. Instead strive to be the best you can be without measuring yourself against anyone and being wrong means you're human.

40. When you stop judging others you will learn to accept them for who they are thus you begin to accept yourself just as you are.

41. Your past is a part of who you are but it does not determine who you will become. Let go and be free or keep holding on and be miserable.

42. Take out a new canvas everyday and start over. Yesterday is gone and is a memory. Tomorrow may never come and is a dream. Today is all you have and it is a blessing.

43. Every day you have a choice to stay captive or you can be brave and take out your courage key and unlock your life. Stop wallowing in "what if" and begin basking in your bravery.

44. Look for at least one opportunity each day to grow and evolve. Read a new book, write in your journal, it doesn't matter what it is as long as it takes you one step closer to fearless living.

45. Get over yourself! Someone out there has it worse than you. While you are important indeed, the world does not revolve around you.

46. Fearless living is about survival of the fittest. Either you change, grow and evolve or life will pass you by. Get up and get into your life.

47. You can't change everything in your life in one choice, but the choice to live fearlessly can dramatically change your life.

48. Choose to live deliciously! Write down your recipe for a delicious life on a real recipe card. Get creative and add in a little spice, passion, excitement, satisfaction and zest and you are sure to whip up a life that makes your mouth water.

49. Clock in and go to work! Living fearlessly is an inside job. It's the most important job you will ever work in your life. Go in early, work hard, take on extra projects, be on the leadership team, put in 100%, stay late, clock out and start all over again. When you work this job like it's the only one you'll ever have the recognition, raises and promotions are guaranteed.

50. You are the Genie you've been waiting for! Discover her, release her, trust her and protect her. Decide what you want, how you want to be and how you want to live your life and get it, be it and live it. The only thing keeping you from living a rewarding and fulfilling life is you. Tell your ShEgo to get out of the way and allow your SHero to be the queen in your life. It's your life own it, create it, live it and love it—fearlessly!

THE ART OF FEAR-FREE LIVING

6 Week Audio/Video Telecoaching Course

If you desire to deepen your ability to live fear-free, I invite you to participate in my 7-step proven life transformation system The *Art of Fear-Free Living* Audio/Video course. The course is available for you to begin on demand. Each week you will be provided with an audio and video lesson to move through the stages and steps of the program listed below. The program comes with a downloadable workbook and is complete with exercises, action steps, strategies and journal prompt so assist you in learning how to live with more courage and fearlessness. When you are ready to begin your course visit the website below and start your journey.

Step One: Waking Up Your Fears and Defining Your Fearless Life
Step Two: Minding Your Mindset
Step Three: Embrace Your Excuses and Then Eliminate Them
Step Four: Shift Your Mindset on What Really Matters
Step Five: Quieting the Inner Critic and Taking Back Your Power
Step Six: Freeing Your Life by Using Fear to Fuel Your Dreams
Step Seven: Mastering Your Mind and Making it Happen

Start *The Art of Fear-Free Living* course today. Visit my website and let the second round of magic begin. www.catriceology.com

MEET
CATRICE M. JACKSON

*C*ATRICE M. JACKSON, KNOWN ACROSS THE GLOBE AS THE SASSY, SAVVY AND FEARLESS EMPOWERMENT SPEAKER, AMERICA'S DELICIOUS LIFE DESIGNER AND FEAR-FREE LIVING EXPERT IS TAKING THE WORLD BY STORM WITH HER SIGNATURE CATRICEOLOGY KEYNOTE PRESENTATIONS AND COURAGE COACHING STRATEGIES WHIPPED UP TO HELP WOMEN LIVE FEARLESSLY DELICIOUS! CATRICE HAS BEEN INSPIRING AND EMPOWERING WOMEN TO SPEAK AND LIVE THEIR AUTHENTIC TRUTH SINCE 1996 THROUGH KEYNOTE PRESENTATIONS, WORKSHOPS, TELESEMINARS AND ON HER ACCLAIMED RADIO PROGRAM THE FEARLESSLY DELICIOUS LIFE SHOW.

Catrice's is a master expert at helping women face and conquer their fears by awakening their SHero. Catrice is no stranger to fear as she launched her speaking and coaching business in the midst of the recent recession. She's been on a 15 year journey of self-transformation and is passionate not only about living her truth but has dedicated her life to helping other women step boldly into the stilettos of their life and show up and show out.

Catrice is the CEO and Owner of Catriceology Enterprises, a global speaking, coaching and consulting enterprise with a mission to inspire women to live and work fearlessly delicious from the inside out. Catrice is the author of *Soul Eruption! An Amazing Journey of Self-Discovery* and *Delicious! The Savvy Woman's Guide for Living a Sweet, Sassy and Satisfied Life*.

Catriceology is more than a perspective. It's a lifestyle anchored in positive psychology, cognitive behavioral approaches and spiritual principles. Catriceology Enterprises, LLC provides speaking and life designing that's delightfully fresh, innovative, practical and proven to help people discover and awaken their inner Geni(us). Catriceology is a worldwide ministry dedicated to restoring the human spirit through messages of hope, faith and courage. Catrice is a wife, mother and lover of life who has dedicated her life to liberating and empowering women one life at a time. She is a "foodie" who loves to cook, travel, read and help bring dreams to life.

Until we meet again just live your life and make sure it's fearlessly delicious...

Meet the Co-Authors

Linda Joy

Linda Joy, Inspirational Publisher, Conscious Business Catalyst and is dedicated to inspiring women to live deeper, more authentic and inspired lives. She is a passionate advocate for leading, encouraging and inspiring women to rediscover and reconnect with their inner wisdom while providing them with the tips, tools and inspiration to do so. In her twenty year journey from single, welfare mother to award-winning entrepreneur Ms. Joy knows first-hand the power of passion, courage, faith and perseverance in overcoming obstacles to achieve your dreams. Her personal journey encourages and inspires other women to believe in themselves and the power of their dreams and to show them that... anything is possible.

Amy Beth O'Brien

Amy Beth O'Brien, Author, Speaker and Coach encourages women to look at life as a movie, Amy inspires us to star in our own life stories. Through writing, speaking, and coaching, she motivates women to write "life scripts" that are true to our heart's desires, thereby attracting relationships, careers, and lives that are authentic and full of joy. Amy first experienced the power of looking at life as though it were a movie when she found herself stuck in a questionable relationship and needed a way to change her approach. By stepping outside herself and viewing her life from an audience's perspective, she changed her life and began to attract relationships and circumstances true to her own heart.

Dr. Carla Goddard

Dr. Carla Goddard is known as the Sacred Soul Shaman. She draws upon the energetic flow of life to share with people a path to heal their own souls and find the flow of energy in their own lives in order to have profound shifts in awareness. She is a visionary guide, speaker, and author.

Aimee Yawnick

Aimee Yawnick has been mentoring women to make personal growth and development a priority for almost 20 years. By focusing on first things first, Aimee helps her clients build and strengthen their relationship with themselves. Aimee's most recent accomplishment is Co-Authoring the Best Selling women's inspirational anthology, *A Juicy Joyful Life: Inspiration from Women Who've Found the Sweetness In Every Day.*

Angela Shaefers

Producer and host of Your Story Matters radio show, freelance writer and inspirational speaker. She writes various articles on professional networking, inspiration and why our stories matter. She authored her memoir *Grief to Grace*. She speaks and shares her story of healing from shame and fear to discovering her life purpose. Angela positively impacts the world, one story at a time!

Gayle Hall, PhD

Gayle Jopin Hall, is a Psychologist, Counselor, Life Coach, Consultant, Relationship Expert, Business Owner, Professor and Author. She is also President and Founder of DrHallonCall™ as The Happiness Life Coach™. Her goal is to embrace individuals in their own unique way and help them find their Hall Ways to Happiness™ through eclectic coaching methods and behavioral consultations. Gayle believes everyone deserves to live their best life and be happy.

Amethyst Wyldfyre

Amethyst Wyldfyre, The Energy Mastery Coach is a Multidimensional Visionary and Transformational Spiritual Leader, Teacher, Guide and Divine Wisdom Channel. She specializes in serving highly influential systemic change agents, coaches, trainers, speakers, performers, artists and alternative healers to LEAP fearlessly into their highest level of service to the planet.

Christine Pembleton

Christine Pembleton is a proud wife, mother, Companionship Coach, talk show host, author and speaker. With a sincere desire to encourage and empower women who want fulfillment and happiness in their marriages, she helps people understand who God created them to be through her coaching, speaking and writing. In June 2009, Christine released her bestselling book, *Lord, I'm Ready to Be a Wife*, to encourage women who want to get married, and introduce the basics of being a wife. After the international success of her book, Christine started Ready to Be a Wife™, a relationship coaching firm, whose purpose is to equip women with the skills and mindset to enjoy the marriage of their dreams. She conducts teleseminars, workshops and training programs all geared to helping women attract and maintain fulfilling relationships.

Lorna Blake

Lorna Blake has more than 10 years experience helping people take charge of their lives and achieve their goals, Lorna Blake is a powerful and inspiring Empowerment Specialist. She combines her professional training with her own life experiences in coaching her clients. Lorna was recently a featured co-author in The Gratitude Book Project.

Christina Morassi

Christina Morassi is on a mission to unleash wild women to make wild money. She is a former fashion photographer who then got into the healing arts, now she brings them all together to create her own career as a Roaring Business Coach. Christina uses shamanic photography as a tool in her practice to help women embody their inner rock-star.

Shann Vander Leek

Shann Vander Leek, successful television broadcast maven turned international life on your terms accelerator, yogini and author of *Life on Your Terms: The Support You Need to Follow Your Passion From Inspirational Entrepreneurs.* Unconventional and delightfully curious; she is a wildly sought-after transition coach who inspires powerful women in career transition to get focused now, follow their passion and create more balance in their lives. Shann invites you to step on the gas and accelerate your life on your terms with her signature Accelerator Sessions.

CATRICEOLOGY

*C*ATRICEOLOGY IS THE PSYCHOLOGY OF LIVING FEARLESSLY DELICIOUS. CATRICE THROUGH HER PSYCHOLOGICAL EXPERTISE, PASSION FOR EMPOWERING WOMEN AND HER SAVVY, SASSY RECIPES FOR INSPIRING FEARLESS ACTION TEACHES WOMEN HOW TO LIVE FEARLESSLY DELICIOUS ON THEIR OWN TERMS THROUGH COURAGE AND AUTHENTICITY

Catriceology is Catrice's signature concoction of psychological theories, inspired living concepts, practical strategies for growth and big ole dose of common sense. Her favorite flavor of empowerment is a brave blend of candor and compassion. As a fear-free living expert, Catrice holds her clients accountable while holding their hand. As a speaker, Catrice engages on a deep-heart level but keeps it real. As an author Catrice's voice is authentic yet inspiring. As an authentic woman, Catrice M. Jackson lives in integrity, stands confident in her presence and speaks her truth. As an international "fearology" thought leader, Catrice's global vision is to create, cultivate and sustain a world-wide community of brave, bold and confident women who live life fearlessly delicious; a movement where fearless, fierce and fabulous women are FREE to just BE.

Catriceology, an international speaking and coaching enterprise, has one primary intention; to help people go from where they are to where they desire to be. Catrice proudly positions herself as the bridge in people's lives allowing a safe, strong, supportive pathway for the evolution of one's authentic self.

9789108R0015

Made in the USA
Charleston, SC
13 October 2011